JESUS DON'T²
~~WORK~~
FOR THE
IRS

A SPIRITUAL & PERSONAL
PERSPECTIVE OF
THE ORIGINAL GANGSTA
(aka "IRS")

V. AISLEE SMITH, ESQ.
(FORMER MAFIA/IRS CONSIGLIORE)

---

2   "Doesn't"

Jesus Don't Work for the IRS,
A Spiritual And Personal Perspective Of The Original Gangsta
Library of Congress Copyright © 2012 by V. Aislee Smith, Esq.

Disclaimer: This publication provides accurate and authoritative content for informational purposes exclusively. It is sold and purchased with the understanding that the author and the publisher are not rendering legal, tax or accounting representation nor any other professional services, as each individual's circumstances are unique. If legal, tax or accounting expertise is required, please call TaxConcepts, Inc. 404.521.0880 (ATL) or 310.566.7575 (LAX) for a formal consultation.

Please submit inquires for author appearances, interviews and bulk book orders to:

info@ministeroftax.net

Published by:

Minister of Tax, LLC
236 Auburn Avenue
Suite 200
Atlanta, GA 30303
www. TheMinisterofTax.net

Printed and bound in the United States of America
ISBN: 978-1-4675-4180-0

Cover Design and Layout By:
PDG - Pencilworx Design Group, LLC - www.pencilworx.com

Mynidia,

Thnak you 4 ur support & love.

Ur Mmd

Go Get Right.

Dedicated
To:
God

From Whom All Blessings Flow

Thank You

Thank you God for choosing me as "The Minister of Tax" and the vehicle to publish "Jesus Don't Work For The IRS." Why You chose me, I will never know. But I'm sure that You know best.

Momma, there are no words to describe how much I love you and appreciate your sacrifice, dedication, encouragement, character and adventuresome spirit. I will never forget and always cherish our trip to South Africa. Only Boyz II Men could put it better . . . "Mama, I'll always love you."[3]

Dad, thank you for throwing your special swag into this tax thing. I miss you every day. It is so cool having a Father who played saxophone with Jimi Hendrix.[4]

Lauren, thank you for going where you never thought you would go. Thank you for teaching me the art of negotiation. But most importantly, I could not have asked for a better Mother for my son. You are awesome and the smartest woman I know. I love you very much!

Andrew, Daddy loves you so much. If you do nothing else in life, make sure to know God's voice and obey His commands. It's not easy and you will fail. But God will always help you up when you make the first step. He's just waiting on you to believe. Always believe and know that all things are possible through God. All things means all things!

Lisa, I have always admired your tenacity, marketing skills, and beautiful smile. You were always my favorite sister, because you were my only sister. Thank you for believing in me and following God's will to bring me back to the "Dirty South."

---

3 "A Song To Mama" Recorded and released on November 11, 1997. Label: Midtown Records. Written and produced by Babyface.

4 *See* "Electric Ladyland," Track 10 "Rainy Day Dream away. Released October 25, 1968. Recorded Olympic Studios (London) and Record Plant Studios (New York). Producer Jimi Hendrix.

Uncle James, thank you for standing in the gap when Daddy died. Thank you for teaching me that humility is a lifelong venture. Thank you for your words of encouragement. Thank you for prophesying over my life and teaching me to always hold the bar to an unobtainable level so as to always strive for excellence.

Thank you Grandma for your spiritual foundation and for being the rock of our family for so long. Please tell Dad that I said "whassup" and continue to look over us. We all miss you very much.

Thank you Granddad for holding it down on the home front. Thank you for showing your children that Government subsidizes are crutches designed to cripple people from success and wealth.

Mable, we miss you so much. Thank you so much for taking such good care of me. I still can't believe you left us, but I'm sure you're in a better place now. Please ask God to continue to bless and comfort us.

Senator and Mrs. Johnson, thank you for choosing me as the Chairman for the Butler Street YMCA. I am honored and will do my best to uphold our historic legacy.

Thank you to all of my ancestors who marched, bleed, and died just so that I could learn how to read and write. Thank you for showing me the value of the ballot and the knowledge that I come from a great people.

Thank you to Eroca, my Jewish grandmother. Thank you for teaching me the value of history and how essential it is to teach our children our history. More importantly we must make sure our children teach their children their history, never let anyone forget the atrocities that occurred in the past, and do everything in your power to insure that such inhumane mayhem never occurs again.

Thank you Josie for your assistance. I could not have done this without you. You made me a better writer.

Mrs. Tillman, thank you for teaching me that the high road is the right road and the best way to kill a snake is with kindness. Thank you to the

best tax team in the whole world: Mrs. Tillman, Mr. Ancona, Ms. Favors, and Attorney Wood. Your research, analysis, input and support was immeasurable. None of this would have been possible without you. Ms Favors, you are the queen of footnotes. Thank you so much.

Shout outs: Aunt Lorraine, Eric, Julie, Janet, Jimmy, Judy, Duron, Jamie, Chasity, Zion, Caleb, Monique, Aunt Mary, Uncle Therman (The Therminator, we always miss you), JT, Roxie, Jonathan, Joshua, Jay, Jabbar, Keisha, Covi, Uncle Marion, Aunt Christine, Khalil, Christy, Uncle Melvin, Aunt Thelma (Thank you for looking over us. We miss you very much),Vic, Kaitlyn, and Candace.

Shout out to the West Coast Family & Friends.

Thank you to the Omega Psi Phi Fraternity, Inc. and my line brothers (White Boy, KJ, Cahoney, Redd, Bullet Head, Darth Vader, and Heart Murmur). Thank you to Brother Pain, the oldest and outtest neophyte I've ever known. Thank you for showing me the true meaning of brotherhood and character.

Shout out to the BSY Renegades (Althea, Kevin, Al, Rebecca, Jerome, Karlise, Doc, and my Morehouse Bothers Dr. Draper and Dr. Owens). God will bless you for your commitment, dedication and wisdom.

Shout out to Sidrowe (with an "e"). You're one of the most intelligent, wittiest, and coolest Brothers I know. Our "world solving conversations" broaden my perspective and prepared me to write this book.

Shout out to the rest of the Crew: Dex, Bob, Dave, Q & Clay. Enough Said.

Shout out to the Palm Springs Gang: Jimmy, Stacia, Michael, Danny and the Grandkids.

Shout out to LaVon and Annetta from Pencilworx for nailing the cover on the first try. That's right, we do it like Frank Sinatra . . . one take and that's it. Shout out to Michael, Jocelyn, and the rest of the staff. Great Job!

Thank you to EDN Global, Jerome and Alena. You were responsible for establishing the business paradigm for TaxConcepts. We could not have done it without you. Shout out to Alena for giving me the official title of "The Minister of Tax."

To the haters, thank you for your motivation. Every time you laughed, I was more inspired. Every time you sneered, I worked that much harder and smarter. Every time you said that "it couldn't be done," I etched the following words in my mind, heart & soul:

"There are thousands to tell you it cannot be done; there are thousands to prophesize failure. There are thousands to point to you, one by one, the danger that awaits to assail you. With a bit of a grin and a lift of a chin, without any doubting or quitted, just start to sing as you tackle the thing that couldn't be done and you'll do it!"

I'm out.

Peace

V. Aislee Smith, Esq.
The Minister of Tax (J.D., LL.M. (Tax))

TABLE OF CONTENTS

GENESIS

REUBEN

CHAPTER ONE

In the beginning God created the heavens and the earth.[5] And the earth was without form, and void; and darkness was upon the face of the deep. And the Spirit of God moved upon the face of the waters.[6] Who could ever conceive that from this creation the concept of taxes would evolve to a point of consuming our everyday lives?

I was always taught not to discuss politics or religion. Yet, here I am writing about both: Tax and Christianity. How is it that this Black Man, born in Casablanca, Morocco and raised in Savannah, Georgia was called to write about two of the most controversial subjects known to man? *Good Question. Glad you asked.*

Christianity

There's the "Spiritual" part and the "Church"[7] part.

Spiritual

My first spiritual experience was probably at the age of six (6). I distinctly remember learning about the crucifixion of Jesus. I didn't understand why this man had to be beaten, humiliated, and hung on a cross because He proclaimed to be the Son of God. People claim to be God in the streets everyday; yet why was this particular man crucified?

For some reason, in my heart, I wished that I could have taken His place. Little did I know the ignorance of my question. I had no idea the walk this Man would take, so that we could be saved.

Therein began my lesson and journey. Eventually, through my faith, I came to know this Man as the King of Kings and Lord of Lords.

---

5   Genesis 1:1. King James Version (herein after referred to as "KJV").
6   Genesis 1:2 KJV
7   The capitalization of "Church" throughout this book is intentional.

Church

The Church part is easy. As my cousin-in-law always says, when I was growing up, there were two questions that you never heard in my house: *"What do you want for dinner?"* and *"Do you want to go to Church?"*

My sister and I grew up in a sanctified Church in Savannah, Georgia. Excuse me, what was once known as "Sanctified," is now "Pentecostal." It was my Grandmother's Church that would provide the basis for my religious upbringing.

I remember many hymns being sung to the rhythm of metal wash boards played with bent hangers; tambourines ringing with the sounds of Coca-Cola bottle caps; and Church lasting from sun up to sun down.

At Coley Temple, the parishioners believed, if you didn't attend that particular Church, you were going to hell. If a woman wore a dress above her knees, she was going to hell. If a woman wore pants, she was going to hell. The basis for the Church's Christian belief was pure old fashion "fire and brimstone."

Yet, for some reason, even at the age of ten (10), my mind could not conceive that one would go to hell just because they wore the wrong clothing or didn't attend a particular Church. Many Sundays I would pray for my Mom's 1970 Buick Opel Cadet not to start.

From the time we were eating breakfast until the time we got into the car, my silent prayer was consistent. *"Please God, don't let this car start. Please God! Please God!"*

Wow, what an ironic situation, praying to God for the car not to start so that I **didn't** have to go to Church. In all those many years, God only answered my prayer once, but I was grateful nonetheless.

The only thing I can remember about the sermons is the rhythmic nature. The minister always had a member from the congregation read each passage and then he followed in a deep, bellowing southern

preacher's voice. Somewhere along the line the scripture was compared to everyday life and eventually a rip roaring "hoop" would begin.

For the Pentecostal challenged (hereinafter referred to as "PC"), this is a hard one in that I'm really not too sure how to describe it. So, I'll quote a very good friend of mine: "hooping" is when the minister begins to banter and strut like a barnyard rooster spewing words in elongated pronunciations: "Yes" becomes "*Yeahhhhhhhh*" and the congregation becomes deaf, because the minister constantly says: "*I don't think you hear me, Nah!*"

The minister would bring the sermon and congregation to a crescendo and the people would shout up and down the aisles. *Shout?* You know what I mean . . . getting the Holy Spirit inside of you.

Again for the PC, the only way I can describe shouting is if you can imagine how you would react if God's Spirit entered your body; however, your body was unable to contain all of His goodness, mercy glory, and power!

Some Church members would jump uncontrollably, while a group of well-trained ushers surrounded them to ensure that they didn't hurt themselves or anyone else. They would jump until their bodies became limp and eventually lapse into an exhaustive state of unconsciousness.

As a child, the most comical thing was when there were more people shouting than the number of ushers. I would nudge my sister and we would laugh under our breath.

A good day was when the Spirit was so high that someone would "*Run for Jesus.*" That is, while the Choir was singing to the background of rhythmic wash boards and tambourines, and while other Spirit filled members were jumping under the careful watch of well trained ushers, all of a sudden a Church member would get up and start running around the Church in a full sprint!

On those days, only Richard Pryor[8] could put it better . . . *"Holy Jesus, Holy Jesus, what in the world is going on here?"* I would lower my head and snicker to a point of almost uncontainable laughter. Little did I know that one day I would *"Run For Jesus."*

Although I didn't agree with the "fire and brimstone" premise, there could be no doubt that God's Spirit was up in the hizouse[9]. So, I can honestly say that I've known God's Spirit for a long time.

One day, God answered my prayer and we joined St. Matthew's Episcopal Church. St. Matthew's was the complete opposite of Coly Temple. Everybody was laid back; Church lasted two hours max; and the Minister indulged in an occasional libation.

At St. Matthews, I served as an acolyte (alter boy), along with my friends from junior high. We were always so cool. During certain parts of the service, we knew that we had just enough time to run to the store, get some candy, and get back before the benediction.

I remember one time when the twins stole the wine and we all had a good time! *What's the problem?* Jesus' first miracle was turning water into wine.[10] And it was good wine, so I've read.

The fun lasted until I graduated from high school and moved to Atlanta to attend Morehouse College. My spiritual path would take a broad leap when I joined Hillside Chapel and Truth Center. Hillside Chapel taught positive thinking. Every service we would sing:

Our thoughts are prayers
And we are always praying
Our thoughts are prayers

---

8 Richard Franklin Lennox Thomas Pryor was an African American stand-up comedian, actor, social critic, writer and MC. Brother Pryor was especially known for his "uncompromising examinations of racism and topical contemporary issues, which employed colorful vulgarities and profanity, as well as racial epithets. Brother Pryor influences included: Lenny Bruce, Jack Benny, Jonathan Winter, Bill Cosby, Dick Gregory, Redd Foxx & Paul Mooney. *See* Richard Pryor – Wikipedia, the free encyclopedia (http://en.wikipedia.org/wiki/Richard_Pryor) (Retrieved 3.31.12).
9 "house"
10 Cana Wedding Miracle, *See* John 2:1-11. KJV

Be careful what you saying
Think a higher consciousness
A state of peacefulness
And know that God is always there
And every thought becomes a prayer.

Hillside didn't care what kind of clothes you wore or none of that. Cool, I can finally wear jeans to Church. I always believed that God looks at your heart and not your clothes, car or home.

However, for some reason, when my Mom and I went to Church, she would always apologize for my attire. *"I did the best I could and he's a grown man now."* I would just give her a hug and kiss her on the forehead.

Hillside's spiritual leader is Dr. Barbara King. Dr. King is a beautiful Black Woman with a hug that will make you feel like you're home. I'm certain that she was destined for greatness, because her presence is so strong.

God had to make her seven feet tall, because a smaller frame could not hold all of His talents, gifts and love. (Even though she may not be seven feet, she seems like it.)

Church was held in a small chapel, holding about five hundred people and attendance was growing at an increasing rate. When you walked through the door your eyes were immediately affixed on twelve (12) huge multi-colored keys. Each key represented a spiritual gift. You see, we all have spiritual gifts and it's up to us to recognize them and utilize them for the benefit of God and mankind. [11]

No more praying to God for the car not to start. I was actually excited and enjoyed what I was learning. It was right down my alley. No fire and

---

11   1 Corinthian 12:1-13. KJV.

brimstone and did I mention I could wear jeans? *"It was on like Donkey Kong."*[12]

Little did I know that Hillside was establishing the foundation for the spiritual path that I was about to embark upon. Now was the time to embrace the positive and to eradicate negative thinking. It was time to take the game up another notch. It was the beginning of wearing the armor of God and engaging in spiritual warfare.[13]

At Hillside, I discovered that one of my spiritual gifts is faith. Faith is the substance of things hoped for and the evidence of things unseen.[14] *"What in the world are you talking about?"*

Faith is seeing the unseen when everything you see seems futile. Faith is using your visionary skills and seeing that God has a golden nugget in every circumstance that seems unconquerable. Faith is a million people saying, *"we can't do it"* and you saying *"there is always a way with God."* Faith is knowing, that you know, that God has your back.

Disclaimer: Having your back may not be the way you want or even anticipated, but ultimately God has your back. He won't let any hurt, harm or danger come to you.

This foundation would ultimately come full circle, because I was also exposed to tithing and the benefits therein. I believe in tithing, because the Bible says that God will bless you, if you tithe.[15]

"Excuse me, did you say that God will bless you, as in letting good things happen to you if you tithe?" "You Got It!" *"Well Count Me In."* Is this self centered? Maybe. But for some reason God's blessings "jus feel so gud."[16]

---

12 "Donkey Kong" is a franchise video games series featuring a large ape called "Donkey Kong". Creator Shigeru Miyamoto. Developers: Nintendo, Rare, Namco, Paon, Retro Studios. Publishers: Nintendo. First released July 9, 1981. (Cite received from Donkey Kong – Wikipedia, the free encyclopedia, http://en.widipedia.org/wiki/Donkey_Kong).

13 Ephesians 6:12. KJV
14 Hebrews 11:1. KJV
15 Malachi 3:10 KJV
16 "Just Feels So Good"

As I said, during this time I was in college, so initially, my income was not substantial. However, later I would discover the wonderful world of tithing and tax. Therein would begin one of my greatest journeys.

Today, I attend Impact Church, D.C.D. (Doing Church Differently) in Atlanta, GA. And boy do they mean "Doing Church Differently." Church lasts one hour and you don't feel like you missed a thing. We don't have a choir. We have a band and our band can play everything from "When I Think of the Goodness of Jesus" to Miles Davis' "Flamenco Sketches" to Bird's "Take Five."

Olu Brown is our head servant leader. The first time that I saw him I knew that it was going to be okay. If the minister is wearing jeans, then I know dog gone skippy that it's okay for me to wear jeans.

Our sermons are filled with practical applications, community service projects and connection groups. I knew this was the place for me when Olu asked the members to support another new Church by attending its inaugural service. Then he said: ". . . and if God inspires you to join that Church, then be obedient because it's not about me or Impact, it's about Kingdom business."

In a day when Churches lock their doors to the homeless and emphasize accumulating paper[17] rather than saving souls, it is refreshing to belong to a Church that really gets it.

Our congregation is growing exponentially and I invite you to attend or listen on-line. See www.impact.dcd.org. Now that we got the Christianity part out of the way, let's talk about the tax side.

TAX

How did I become "The Minister of Tax?" Well that part is a little more complicated. Tax, what a calling! It had to be a calling, because I dare

---

17 "money"

say that no one wakes up in the morning to the smell of grits with cheese for breakfast and runs to their Mother saying:

Son: *"Mommy, Mommy, I know what I want to be when I grow up."*

Mom: "Son, what do you want to be?"

Son: *"I wanna be a tax attorney."*

Mom: "That's good Son. You can do anything you want as long as you put your mind to it."

Not! Actually, when I was growing up, I thought that I wanted to be an oceanographer until later I realized that I just really wanted to go scuba diving.

My only memory of tax was completing a Form 1040EZ and understanding why the name was "EZ." It truly was so "easy." *"Well, how did you become a tax attorney?"*

After graduating from Windsor Forest High School, in Savannah, Georgia, I had no idea what career I wanted to pursue. After taking the ASVAB military test, I displayed a high aptitude for computer science. During the late seventies, computers were the latest and greatest upcoming career. Seemed like a great fit.

I was accepted to Morehouse College and continued to do well in computer science until my junior year. It was during this year that I had an epiphany. I realized that computers were too impersonal for my personality; so I changed my major to business and decided to pursue law school.

During this year, another major event occurred. I decided to pledge a fraternity, Omega Psi Phi, Inc. If we ever have the opportunity to meet, you'll find that I am straight across the board. That is, what you see is what you get. Thus, I can candidly state that I did not initially pledge

my fraternity because of brotherhood, community service or any other reputable factor.

There was a pledge line called the "Clone 10." They were participating in a step show in the gymnasium. Standing room only and it was their turn to step. The lights went off and when they reappeared, there were ten pledges clothed with white linen coverings in perfect formation from the shortest to the tallest.

Then suddenly from front to back, each one tore off their covering in a synchronized pattern and they were wearing black tuxedos with bald heads. The crowd went wild, the women screamed and immediately I knew that this was the fraternity for me!

Later, I discovered that I would cultivate some of the best friends that I would ever have in my life. Moreover, my experiences would prove to establish a foundation that would affect me greatly.

When I pledged there were eight of us known as the "AE-8[18]". However, with the good sometimes comes the bad. The bad was . . . I lost my mind. After pledging, instead of majoring in business, I majored in women, drinking, and fraternizing, cum lade, Phi Beta Kappa.

It was also during this time that I discovered that I had a special talent. I found out that I could cram extremely well. You see, I never attended classes; however, I would study my assets off the night before an exam and I would get the highest grade in the class. Thereby, leading to an inevitable and most logical question . . . *"Why go to class when you can cram and still get an "A. It just don't make sense."*

Life has a way of teaching lessons and this lesson was taught via my marketing class professor. Marketing was an one (1) hour class and when I did show up for class, emphasis on "did," I was at least twenty minutes late. *Key point!*

---

18   Also known as "the 8 GGs."

I would walk in the class with my fraternity jacket, collar thrown up, strutting in a most arrogant manner, no book, no paper, and holding a Burger King cup. Inside of the cup was Jack Daniels and Coke. *"Yeah, I was a bad boy!"*

After finding an available seat and casually asking another classmate for a piece of paper[19], I would carelessly doodle on the paper and promptly leave when class ended.

Yet, when it was time for exams, I would again study my assets off. I got the highest grade on the midterm, the second highest grade on the final, and never scored less than a ninety-five (95) on any exam. At the end of the semester, I confidently walked up to the Wailing Wall to check out my grade and, to my shock and surprise, I received a "D."

I checked my exam number several times and the results were always the same "D." I immediately made a straight edge out of a loose piece of paper, placed the straight edge on my exam number and carefully followed it across and again the results were the same, a big fat "D." And anybody who knows anything knows that you cannot change a "D" into any legitimate grade.

"Surely there's a mistake, I never scored less than a ninety-five (95) on any exam." I approached the professor in complete disbelief and asked about the gross miscalculation that had occurred:

> *"Well, Mr. Smith, although you did extremely well on my exams, I also gave daily quizzes that were worth thirty-five percent (35%) of your grade and you received a zero. Moreover, it is obvious from your stellar exam performance that you are more than capable of doing the math and even if you scored one hundred (100) on every exam, that would still leave you with a sixty-five (65). Oh, by the way, because this class is in your major, a passing grade of seventy (70) or above is required. So, I guess I'll see you next year. Have a great day!"*

---

19 A Morehouse Man always carries a pen."

Needless to say you could have knocked me over with a feather. I was floored. The next year the class was taken up a notch. Actually, it was downright hard. *You Think!* Although my attendance was up from the previous year, I didn't score "A"s on all of my exams and candidly, I deserved a "B," despite the fact that I received an "A." I think I received the "A" that I deserved the year before.

Hindsight is always "20/20." In hindsight I am thankful for the life lesson, because I learned more about myself than any marketing class could ever teach me.

In the interim, while I was partying full-time and studying part-time, the money ran out and I had to employ a different strategy. I couldn't ask my Mother for any additional money, so it was time to go to work and go to work I did.

I would work for a semester and attend school for a semester. I intentionally took jobs that I knew I would not enjoy. That way, I would not be tempted to stay and abandon my goal of law school.

As a result, I worked in every major hotel in Atlanta, including: the Ritz Carlton (Buckhead & Downtown); Westin Peachtree Plaza; Marriott Marquis; Hilton; and Hyatt. I worked as a front desk clerk, life guard, banquet waiter, room service waiter, golf greens keeper and even a security guard. I called it a *"legitimate hustle."*

The summer was reserved for maniac months. A typical summer day was as follows:

10:30 a.m. – 3:30 p.m.	Post Office Clerk
4:30 p.m. – 10:30 p.m.	Hotel Banquet Waiter
11:30 p.m. – 7:30 a.m.	Fork Lift Driver

Many people rightfully warn against texting and e-mailing while driving; yet, I transformed changing clothes while driving into an art. During these summer months, I made as much money as I could and kept a part-time job when school started.

Trust me! When you work maniac hours, I guarantee that two things will happen: 1) you will save money and 2) you will lose weight. When sleep becomes a priority over eating and spending money, then you will notice an increase in your bank account and a decrease in your weight.

My family often accuses me of being part West Indian, because I would work so many jobs simultaneously. In my family, I invented the eighty (80) hour work week. But of course, when I was a young man, I could work all day and party all night.

But I never gave up. I later remember sharing my desire to go to law school with the same marketing professor and his reply was, *"you're still chasing that pipe dream."* I merely nodded in the affirmative and, fueled by his words, I hit the books even that much harder. For God determines my destiny . . . not man.

After graduation, because of my "unique situation," few law schools were willing to take a chance with me. *Unique situation?* Yes, "unique situation." I started a four (4) year undergraduate degree in 1978 and completed in 1987. Let's see that's 4, 5, 6, 7, 8, 9 years. *Wozi, Wozi, Wozi.*

I did well on the LSAT-excellent in some areas, but not overall outstanding. It's challenging to excel on an entrance exam when you're working maniac hours. Yet my mantra remained the same . . . **Stick to the plan!**

I continued to accept jobs that I didn't like so that I wouldn't be tempted to become content; get in debt; and relinquish a goal that I had been pursuing for so long. Interestingly enough, the last jobs I had were a fire dispatcher, a roofer and a waiter.

At this point in my life, I was convinced that I could either: think my way out of; talk my way out of; or charm my way out of any situation. Despite all of the challenges, I was determined that law school was not gonna evade me like a greased pig at the country fair.

However, one day the unexpected and unavoidable occurred . . . I got tired and I gave up. *Tired! Tired! Tired!* I decided that it was time for me to purse a finance position, purchase a home and car and begin a real life. It was at this time that God stepped in and said, "Now that you've tried everything that you could do, let me show you what I can do!"

After receiving numerous denial letters, there was one law school left, Howard University School of Law. The time had long passed for notification and I still had not received a letter. While working at the Savannah Fire Department, I distinctly remember saying "*if you're going to deny me, then you're going to tell me to my expletive face!*"

So, I called the admission office still some kind of hot, but my Momma "ain't raise no fool." When the representative picked up the phone, I asked,

"*When will you begin to accept applications for the next law school class?*"

The representative said, "what's your name?"

"*I just need to know when I can submit another application.*"

"What's your name sir?"

"*My name is Aislee Smith.*"

"Just one moment, (intentional pause), well sir, you've been accepted and your acceptance letter was returned because of an undeliverable address. We're really glad you called."

"*Excuse me Ma'am, could you please repeat yourself?*"

I was happier than a pig in three day old slop. I fell on my knees and thanked God. Finally the wait was over. Little did I know that a whirlwind was about to begin.

I began Howard University School of Law in 1987 ready to become a corporate attorney. It was a natural progression. I love business, business loves me. *Cool.* However, in my second year I took a class that changed my life forever.

Every second year law student is required to take "Federal Income Taxation" taught by Professor Boyer. Professor Boyer was like most law school professors: arrogant, obnoxious, and intimidatingly[20] smart.

I remember, on the first day of class, Professor Boyer was discussing whether reimbursed insurance proceeds qualified as a deductible medical expense. In an effort to test/trick the class, he described the scenario and drew a flow chart of the transaction on the chalk board. While Professor Boyer was diagramming the transaction, I noticed what appeared to be a miscalculation. I semi-confidently raised my hand.

"Yes, Mr. Smith."

"Professor Boyer, your calculations appear to be in error." (Note: Emphasis on "appear.")

The entire class looked at me as if I were personally responsible for the deaths of Jesus Christ, Malcolm X, Martin Luther King, Jr., and Mahatma Gandhi.

"Are you sure Mr. Smith?"

"Yes, Professor Boyer, I am sure."

To the surprise of the class, Professor Boyer agreed and complimented me on my analysis. From that day on, I knew that I was destined to be the "Tax Man."

---

20   According to spell check, intimidatingly is not a word, but I sure do like the way it sounds.

Tax Man [21]

One, two, three, four . . .
(guitar riff)

Let me tell you how it will be
There's one for you, nineteen for me.
'Cause I'm the taxman,
Yeah, I'm the taxman.

Should five per cent appear too small,
Be thankful I don't take it all.
Cause I'm the taxman,
Yeah, I'm the taxman.

If you drive a car, I'll tax the street;
If you try to sit, I'll tax your seat;
If you get too cold, I'll tax the heat;
If you take a walk, I'll tax your feet.

Taxman!

'Cause I'm the taxman,
Yeah, I'm the taxman.
Don't ask me what I want it for,
        (ah-ah, Mister Wilson)
If you don't want to pay some more.
        (ah-ah, Mister Heath)

'Cause I'm the taxman,
Yeah, I'm the taxman.
Now my advice for those who die, (taxman)
Declare the pennies on your eyes. (taxman)

---

21 "Taxman." Song by the Beatles from the Revolver Album. Released: August 5, 1966. Genre: Blues, rock, hard rock. Writer: George Harrison. Producer: George Martin. *See* Taxman – Wikipedia, the free encyclopedia ("http://enwikipedia.org/wiki/Taxman)(Retrieved 3.31.12).

'Cause I'm the taxman,
Yeah, I'm the taxman.
And you're working for no one but me.

Taxman!

During the semester, for some reason, tax came as easy as breathing. The Internal Revenue Code and Treasury regulations were like reading Grimm's Fairy Tales. Needless to say, I was the tax man and everybody wanted to be my friend.

It was not until my third year that I discovered that I was a man on an island. Tax is not a popular subject at Ivy League Law Schools and you can surely believe that it's not popular at African-American Law Schools.

But there was one professor who taught the only two advanced tax courses at Howard University Law School, Professor Loretta Argrett. I would have taken her tax class even if I didn't like tax and twice on Sundays.

Don't trip, I was not the only one. All of the guys had a crush on Professor Argrett. She eventually served with the Justice Department as Secretary of Tax during President Clinton's Administration. Professor Argrett put the finishing touches on my crude analysis and heightened my desire to become a tax attorney.

You see, there are basically two ways to become a tax attorney: 1) work for a large firm that is willing to give you the tax experience; or 2) go back to law school and pursue a Master's in Law specializing in tax. The only law schools providing LL.M (Tax) degrees during the time were: New York University, Georgetown University Law Center, and University of Florida.

Well unfortunately, the first option was not available because the tax world is dominated almost exclusively by white males. Moreover, I later discovered that it was way too easy to say "no" to a single chocolate

attorney, because there was no one beating down the door insisting upon fair play.

However, as our elders always say. . . "But God!" God created a tax fellowship just for me. I was blessed with the opportunity to work for the premiere tax authority, the Internal Revenue Service and they paid for my LL.M. at Georgetown. *Wow, ain't God so much better than good. He's awesome!*

This was the beginning of the beginning. I worked as a tax attorney, specializing in Internal Revenue Code §501(c)(3) tax-exempt organizations and, in the evening, I attended classes at Georgetown and studied tax on the weekend. *Wow, what an exciting life.* During this time, the only song that could adequately describe my life is by the Police, "Too Much Information, Running Through My Head, Too Much Information, Driving Me Insane. [22]"

Yet, with each passing day, my net worth was increasing exponentially. After working with the IRS for ten (10) years and receiving a Masters of Laws degree specializing in tax, it was time for me to go.

I accepted a manager's position with PricewaterhouseCoopers in the New York/New Jersey region. During the time, PricewaterhouseCoopers was the number one accounting firm in the nation. Only one problem, PricewaterhouseCoopers didn't specialize in health care tax law and during the time, I was convinced that health care tax was the way to go.

Most of my friends were doctors and they were making money. My friends that were pharmaceutical representatives were making money. Hell, even the health equipment sales people were making money. So, I was determined that health care tax was going to be my angle.

After working for two (2) years with PricewaterhouseCoopers, I eventually got my shot. I was offered a position with Ernst & Young located on 50th & 7th, NYC. Eventually, the firm moved to Times Square.

---

22 "Too Much Information" by the Police. Ghost In the Machine (album), Released October 2, 19881. Label: A&M, Producers: The Police & Hugh Padgham.

It was so cool. In the evening after work, I would flow from the streets into a bar and have a great time. And the free entertainment! Walking down the street and checking people out. *It don't get no better.*

I was a manager for two partners. One was the brains and the other could smootz his assets off. I clocked them both and learned invaluable lessons.

I'm chillin[23] in the NYC; sittin[24] in fat box seats at Yankee baseball games on the firm's money with waitresses and an American Express credit card in hand; meeting my wife on Friday nights for dinner and a Broadway show; taking clients to Knicks games; God is even about to bless us with a child; yeah man life is all gud[25]. All of a sudden God shows up again.

> **"Son, you always wanted your own firm. Now is the time."**

> *"No it's not God. My wife is pregnant; I haven't saved any money; and I'm having a great time. Trust me, Now Is Not The Time."*

> **"Yes, it is."**

> *"No it isn't."*

> **"Yes, it is."**

> *"No it isn't."*

Sound familiar? "Stop laughing, it's not funny."

Ironically, after my conversation, all of a sudden, my cases began to dry up like the Sahara Desert during the dry season and the partners were

---

23 "relaxing"
24 "sitting"
25 "good"

looking at me like I grew three heads and one of them was sticking out of my butt.

Then, I was placed on a special project, "Entrepreneur of the Year Award." Every year, Ernst & Young honors the top entrepreneurs and it was my responsibility to interview the companies and make the appropriate recommendations.

Sounds good, right? Wrong. Interviewing successful CEOs does not constitute billable hours and if you don't make it rain with billable hours, then you're expendable.

So here I am, waiting for this CEO from a multimillion dollar company to arrive and I have another talk with God.

> *"God, why do you have me here when you know that I need to generate billable hours?"*

> **"As I said, now is the time to start your firm and by the way, you're an idiot."**

> *"An idiot! Why am I an idiot?"*

> **"You're getting ready to start your business, whether you like it or not and I have blessed you by placing some of New York's most successful CEOs at your very feet. You now have the ability to ask them any question you like and because they're coveting this award so badly, they will answer your question with zeal, a coke and a smile."**

The proverbial light bulb is about to break, because it's glowing so brightly over my head. Trust me, an attorney's first nature is to analyze and asking questions is not far behind.

Ladies and gentlemen, in this corner you have one soon-to-be entrepreneur and in the other corner you have a successful CEO who wants the coveted "Entrepreneur of the Year" award. Let's get ready to rumble!

1. So when did you realize that you wanted to operate your own firm?
2. What was the most challenging aspect of becoming an entrepreneur?
3. How did you raise the capital?
4. How do you handle your competition?
5. How, What, When, Where, and Why?

Finally, I accepted the fact that it was time for me to leave. One day, I was driving into Manhattan and I was stalled because of traffic at the Lincoln Tunnel and God asked,

"What was the first job that you ever had?"

"I was a bag boy at Food Town[26] *in Savannah, Georgia on Ogeechee Road."*

"Where are you working now?"

"I'm working for Ernst & Young in Manhattan in Times Square."

Food Town was the first job you ever had and Ernst & Young is the last job that you will ever have."

When I arrived at the office, one of the partners was waiting for me with a disgruntled look on his face. "Aislee, this is really killing me and I hate to do this." *"Dude, let's cut the pomp and circumstance and get to the chase."*

He looked at me like I was out of my mind. What he failed to realize is I had God on my side and I was moving to bigger and better things. Side

---

26 "Food Town" is now "Kroger."

Note: Sometimes God lets you fall so you can get back up.
When God says He will only give you as much as you can bear, on occasion I would like to have some semblance of input, because sometimes we don't always share the same sense of humor. But, I can honestly say that He has never failed me nor forsaken me.

On that day I made a very logical decision. We owned property in Washington, DC: it seemed like the perfect place to begin my business. Let's move there.

Entrepreneur Rule #1: You Eat What You Kill!

Before starting my own business, I was a tax snob. My clients included the Roman Catholic Church, Montefori Hospital, Beth Israel Hospital, and other multimillion dollars clients. Thus, my knowledge and exposure were beyond reviewing or preparing mere personal income taxes.

Many times, my friends and family would ask me to complete their taxes and I would begrudgingly agree with no promise on when I could return them. You see, personal income taxes are not sexy and actually, they are beneath my vast araldite tax knowledge.

When you start your own, the attitude completely changes. *"Yes Sir, we do personal income taxes and we do them very well."*

I started my legitimate hustle all over again. I met clients at Georgetown University's Law Library; at Starbucks; or at their home if necessary. Doing my best . . . to getter[27] done.

The next winter, we had a record breaking snow season. I shoveled twenty inches of snow on Wednesday, so that I wouldn't have to shovel forty-five on Thursday. Shoveling snow was no longer fun nor could I view it as exercise. As a matter of fact, I now understand why people have heart challenges when they shovel snow. It was at this time that I realized it was time to go.

---

27 "get it"

Coincidentally (yeah, right), about this time my sister called and asked if I were interested in leasing an office in Atlanta. I told her "thanks; but no thanks." Don't get me wrong, Atlanta is a wonderful place; however, I'm trying to live in a city where it's warm all of the time. She asked me to just consider it and I told her that I would.

Two weeks later, I flew to Atlanta, walked into the office and felt God moving. *"God I can't believe that you want me to move back to Atlanta. I've had too many great times here, too many challenging memories and too many wild times."*

Yet, here I am back in Atlanta, ready to begin my career as an entrepreneur. Therein lay, the genesis of "TaxConcepts, LLC."

Coming from the IRS, PricewaterhouseCoopers and Ernst & Young, I felt more than ready. The IRS provided the technical expertise, culture and degree, L.L.M. (Tax); while PricewaterhouseCoopers and Ernst and Young polished my customer service skills and took the tax analysis up another notch. *"Thank you God. I'm ready."*

During those days, if I made one hundred and fifty dollars ($150.00), I was happy. One day, a young lady came into the office to have her taxes prepared. I politely asked her what her filing status was last year and she replied: *"Single, head of household, I don't know. You see, I had a baby from this man and he took all of the money out of my bank account and left me to raise our child alone."* Then she began to cry.

My initial internal response was, *"Whoa Nelly! I'm not prepared for this."* I didn't even have a napkin, let alone a box of tissue. Then God informed me that not only did I have a tax firm but I also had a ministry.

This was another crossroad in the scheme of His divine plan. The most unusual looking tax attorney encompassing God's word into the Internal Revenue Tax Code. Trust me, when I attend tax legal educational classes, there "ain't be"[28] too many minorities.

---

28 "are not"

I've always been taught that God is everywhere and He is. He's in the sky and He's in the earth. He's in you and He's in me.

Well, if God is in the Internal Revenue Code, then He must truly be everywhere and in everything. Thus, it had to be my calling, because no one in their right mind would pursue a subject matter so complex and confront the IRS every single day.

Yet, this is what God has called me to do and I shall do my best. That's how I became the Tax Man, a.k.a. the Minister of Tax.

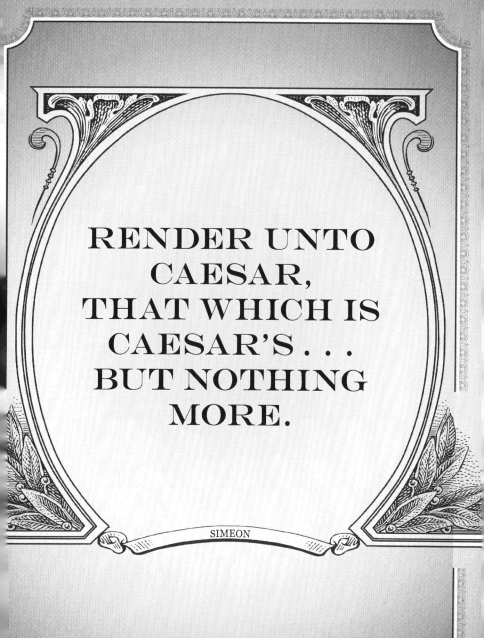

RENDER UNTO CAESAR, THAT WHICH IS CAESAR'S . . . BUT NOTHING MORE.

SIMEON

CHAPTER TWO

And the chief priests and the scribes the same hour sought to lay hands on him; and they feared the people: for they perceived that he had spoken this parable against them.[29]

And they watched him, and sent forth spies, which should feign themselves just men, that they might take hold of his words, that they might deliver him unto the power and authority of the governor.[30] And they asked him, saying, Master, we know that thou sayest and teachest rightly, neither acceptest thou the person of any, but teachest the way of God truly:[31]

Is it lawful for us to give tribute unto Caesar, or no?[32] But [Jesus][33] perceived their hypocrisy[34] and craftiness, and said unto them, Why tempt ye me?[35] Show me a penny. Whose image and superscription hath it? They answered and said, Caesar's.[36]

And he said unto them, Render therefore unto Caesar the things which be Caesar's, and unto God the things which be God's. . . .[37]

From a biblical perspective, it is unequivocally clear that Jesus Christ commands all Christians to pay their taxes. More astoundingly, this principle is not restricted to Christians, Jews, Muslims, or Buddhists. It is not restricted to Black, White, Red or Yellow races. Age is irrelevant and even social security and other retirement income is taxed.

As a matter of fact, you don't even have to be a United States citizen to pay taxes.[38] Amongst the entire religious, social, race, nationality and/or age differences, as Americans, we all share the common thread that we

---

29 Luke 20:19 KJV

30 *Id.* at 20.

31 *Id.* at 21

32 *Id.* at 22.

33 Added for clarification.

34 Matthew 22:15, KJV

35 Luke 20:23 KJV

36 *Id.* at 24.

37 *Id.* at 25.

38 *See* Taxation of Nonresident Aliens, http://www.irs.gov/businesses/article/ (Retrieved April 6, 2010).

are all subject to the authority of the Internal Revenue Service.
We've always heard that love brings people together. Maybe we've
missed the boat. It appears as though it is the Internal Revenue Service
that brings us all together, because the vast majority of men, women
and applicable children in these United States "Render Unto Caesar that
which is Caesar's."

Let me present this query . . . if we as a nation did not believe in
"Rendering Unto Caesar," why is it that every 15th of April our Post
Offices are overcome with throngs of people standing in boa constrictor
lines waiting for the precious post mark indicating that Caesar's paper
was properly filed in a timely manner.

When I was working for the IRS in Washington, D.C., I would park at the
Union Station Post Office and watch the people run to the Post Office in
a panic to insure they filed their taxes on time. Actually, I wanted to hold
up a huge sign and let everyone know you can file an online extension
that is good until October 15th.

*You're kidding me. I can really submit a single sheet of paper or press a
"send" button on the computer and the IRS will let me file an extension
that is good until October 15th. Get outta here!*

Believe it or not, if an extension is properly and timely filed, you have
until October 15th to file your Form 1040 US Individual Tax Return.
However, don't be fooled! If you owe taxes, the interest time clock begins
ticking until the entire tax liability is ultimately paid.

Yet amidst all of this cosmic unity, rendering unto Caesar that which is
Caesar's is only half the story. If we are suppose to pay our taxes; then
we are also expected to abide by the rules and regulations promulgated
to ensure the proper assessment and collection of such taxes.

However, in the writings of Jesus Christ, neither Mark, Matthew, Luke,
or John reported that any additional actions were necessary other than
giving Caesar his just due. Moreover, I would propose that there is

no such declaration in the Torah, Koran, or the Universal Doctrine of Atheism (if any such document exists).

As self-proclaimed "Minister of Tax," I am proposing that all citizens (Christian, Islam, Jewish, etc.) adopt the mantra of

"Render unto Caesar that which is Caesar's . . . But Nothing More."

This mantra is one of the cornerstones of our firm. The IRS is entitled to receive all of the appropriate taxes they are due; however, every individual is also entitled to take every deduction that is legally available. Although this concept is not novel, for some reason, this notion evades the majority of Americans.

One of the primary challenges is our complex tax system. Our tax rules are so convoluted and complicated that most Americans are completely oblivious to how they operate. *How can anyone possibly expect to understand a system that is so vast and so complex?*

Perhaps, this is precisely the point. If one does not understand the system, how can one possibly challenge it? Thus, if one cannot challenge the system, then the compliance rate increases exponentially and our government will continue to reap more than its fair share of taxes.

This complex subject matter is accompanied by a plethora of tax preparers who are inept, unprofessional, uncompassionate, and unintelligible. Since leaving the private and public work sector, the atrocities that I have witnessed have made me cringe.

Early in the game, I distinctly remember reviewing a return from a major national tax firm and asking myself . . . is it that they *"don't know"* or *"don't care?"*

This is what "had happen[39]." A taxpayer made a charitable noncash property contribution to the Salvation Army and received a receipt.

---

39   "happened"

(Lesson No. 1: Always keep your receipts. At an audit, it's not what happened, it's what you can prove.)

The taxpayer contributed the following items:

1. One (1) Dell laptop computer
2. One (1) Panasonic 42" flat screen television
3. Broyhill Dining Room Suite with eight (8) chairs, Hutch, and China Cabinet
4. Several large bags of clothes and
5. A Lazy Boy Recliner

When making charitable contributions, the Internal Revenue Code allows us to choose between several valuation methods. "Thrift Store" is the lowest value and "Comparable Sales" is the highest. Once a method is chosen, we can deduct the appropriate value.[40] On the return, the aforementioned items were recorded with a fair market value of five hundred dollars ($500.00). Selah.[41] (Intentional Pause)

Good Question and I'm glad you asked. Clearly the value of the items contributed was more than five hundred dollars ($500.00), so why was it misrepresented on the tax return?

Noncharitable contributions are reported on the Schedule A and there is some small writing that states: "If the amount is over five hundred dollars ($500), complete Form 8283."

Form 8283 is a fairly straight forward document. The Service just wants to know:

1. Who did you give it to?

---

40   Depending on the type of charitable organization, the contribution is limited to fifty percent (50%) or thirty percent (30%) of your adjusted gross income. *See* Internal Revenue Code §170(b).
41   "Pause." *See* Selah – Wikipedia, The Free Encyclopedia (http://en.wikipedia.org/wiki/Selah) (Retrieved 3.20.2012). Used frequently in the Hebrew Bible, often in the Psalms and is a difficult concept to translate. The most concise definition is "Let those with eyes see and with ears hear" [citation needed] [sic]. Selah notes a break in the song and as such is similar in purpose to Amen in that it stresses the importance of the preceding passage.

2. Where did you give it?

3. Which valuation method did you utilize (comparable sales, thrift value, etc.)[42].

Rather than complete the Form, the preparer carelessly inputs five hundred dollars ($500.00) and the return is finished. "Next."

Candidly, in the beginning I was befuddled. I'm not the sharpest knife in the drawer, but after awhile, it hit me . . . "The Cattle Theory." *"Get 'em in, then get 'em out."* The more we do the more we get and the more we get the more money we make. (*See,* "The World is Filled With Pimps & Hustlers").

On the opposite end of the tax professional spectrum, there are the pimps who comprehend a little bit of tax knowledge and market it in a convincing fashion. They are normally in the business for a quick buck and have more of a hustler approach.

In our situation, the client was somewhat fortunate, because the error did not result in an increase in tax liability. That is, he paid more in taxes than he was legally obligated. However, what happens when the mistake yields an errant awesome refund that during the time was nothing but a "blessing from God?"

Those Who Don't Know

For those who don't know, the game is fairly short. After filing the errant form or transaction, the IRS will contact the taxpayer approximately one year later, informing them of the error(s). Of course this letter is accompanied by his two favorite mob brothers, "Tony" and "Sal," also known as "Interest" and "Penalties."

After the IRS shows up with Tony and Sal, the original tax preparer normally disappears and leaves the client high and dry. Under most circumstances, the client settles with the IRS and normally pays an

---

42 Comparable Sales yields the highest value and thrift shop value yields the lowest value.

unnecessarily exorbitant amount of taxes, interest and penalties through a monthly installment agreement. Meanwhile the hustler moves on to the next victim.

Those Who Don't Care

For those who don't care, the story is a little different. Most of those who "don't care" know the law; hence, errant returns are rarely filed. Because they "don't care," they lack the professionalism and compassion to go the extra step and make sure that you are rendering to Caesar only what you owe and nothing more.

One of the most invaluable lessons I learned from Ernst & Young was "take care of the client and not your pocket." That is, counsel your client with proper advice, even if it means that you do not benefit from it financially. Your client will respect you more and you will develop a relationship instead of conducting a singular transaction.

Clearly, this concept escapes those who "don't care." The obscure results of firms that don't care are:

> 1) an extremely conservative return, thereby reducing the chance of an audit (Note: the Internal Revenue Service will rarely audit a return where the Taxpayer is paying more than he/she is legally obligated);

> 2) the amount of refund received is severely minimized or the amount of taxes owed is substantially overstated; and

> 3) the IRS keeps a bonus on the interest-free loan you so graciously provided. (*See*, "The Proverbial Question").

What a wonderful combination--highly complicated laws, combined with a plethora of unknowledgeable and unsympathetic preparers. The Service is well aware of this dichotomy; yet, even when a professional is hired to assist, the taxpayer is still ultimately responsible.

Wait a minute . . . let me get this straight. We are confronted with rocket science; we hire a rocket scientist to build the rocket; the rocket scientist makes a mistake, and we are responsible?

Yet, in spite of this draconian concept, we are expected to "Render Unto Caesar, that which is Caesar's." Ironically, we are expected to obey this rule, in spite of the fact that Caesar is not the ultimate provider. God is the ultimate provider of life, including breath itself. Caesar just gets a cut of what God provides.

Once upon a time; however, it wasn't always like this. There was no "Rendering Unto Caesar." There was only "Render Unto God." The question is, *"Did we choose wisely?"*

Back in the day, (no, not the seventies, way back in the day of the Old Testament) we were governed by Judges instead of Kings. These Judges were chosen by God to interpret His law and do His work.

The book of Judges covers a period of several hundred years following the conquest of Canaan, during which time the people were ruled by individual leaders called "judges" or "saviors."[43] Their task was primarily military, to expel the enemy from the land.

These Judges were strong like Samson[44], fiery like Deborah[45], and some were disbelievers like Gideon[46], who tested God over and over again. And then there was the very last Judge, Samuel.

After generations of being governed by Judges, the "peoples"[47] became restless with God and decided that they wanted to be like everybody else.

---

43   Holy Bible, authorized King James Version, Copyright 1969 by Tyndale House Publishers, Inc., Wheaton, IL 60187.
44   Judges, Chapter 13. New Revised Standard.
45   Judges, Chapter 4, New Revised Standard.
46   Judges, Chapter 6, New Revised Standard.
47   "people"

Back In the Day

Samuel was anointed from birth to serve God.[48] When Samuel grew old, he appointed his sons as Judges for Israel.[49] But his sons did not walk in his ways.[50] They pursued dishonest gain and accepted bribes and perverted justice.[51]

So the elders of Israel gathered together and came to Samuel and said to him, "You are old, and your sons do not walk in your ways, now appoint a king to lead us, like the other nations have."[52]

I imagine that in spite of Samuel's illustrious career, he still felt badly. The Israelites were judged for hundreds of years and, all of a sudden, the people wanted to be ruled by a King. Surely, Samuel questioned himself, his talents, and his devotion.[53]

In the midst of his pain, he prayed to the Lord.[54] And the LORD told him: "Listen to all that the people are saying to you; it is not you they have rejected, but they have rejected me as their king.[55] As they have done from the day I brought them out of Egypt until this day, forsaking me and servicing other gods, so they are doing to you.[56]

Now listen to them, **but warn them solemnly**[57] and let them know what the king who will reign over them will do:[58]

1.   He will take your sons and make them serve with his chariots and

---

48   I Samuel 1:11 New Revised Standard. Samuel's Mother Hannah made a vow with the Lord "[I] f only you will look on the misery of your servant, and remember me, and not forget your servant, but will give to your servant a male child, then I will set him before you as a Nazarite until the day of his death. He shall drink neither wine nor intoxicants, and no razor shall touch his head.
49   *Id.* at 8:1.
50   *Id.* at 8:3.
51   *Id.*
52   *Id.* at 8:4.
53   *Id.* at 8:6. But the thing displeased Samuel when they said, "Give us a king to govern us."
54   Id at 8:6
55   *Id.* at 8:7.
56   *Id.* at 8:8.
57   Emphasis Added.
58   1 Samuel 8 KJV

horses, and they will run in front of the chariots.[59]

2. Some he will assign to be commanders of thousands, and other to plow his ground and reap his harvest, and still others to make weapons of war and equipment for his chariots.[60]

3. He will take a tenth of your grain and your vintage and give it to his officials and attendants[61]

4. He will take a tenth of your flocks, and you yourselves will become his slaves.[62]

5. When the day comes, you will cry out for relief from the king you have chosen and the Lord will not answer you in that day."[63]

Let's take a break here and get the story "sgraight."[64] Samuel told the Israelites that the king would take their sons and make them soldiers to fight the King's battles. Moreover, in fighting these battles, the King will place your sons (and now daughters[65]) on the battle front line, while he governs from afar. *Call me superstitious, but this sounds a little familiar.*

Our beloved King will make the people create "weapons of war." Dare I mention nuclear warfare and any other current weapons that are presently being created? (*Sidebar: Saddam, you are the master illusionist. We still haven't found those weapons of mass destruction*).

And most importantly, the crue de gras, Samuel also told the people that the King would take a tenth of their grains and vintage and give them to his officials and attendants. Every April 15th and October 15th, we all pay taxes to support the most powerful nation in the world.

---

59 *Id.* at 8:11.
60 *Id.* at 8:12.
61 *Id.* at 8:15.
62 *Id.* at 8:17.
63 *Id.* at 8:18.
64 "straight"
65 Although women have served in our military since 1775 by nursing the ill and wounded, laundering and mending clothes and cooking for the troops in camp. In 1993, Secretary of Defense Les Aspin announced a new policy directing the services to train and assign women on combat aircraft and most combat ships. *See* Generations of Women_Moving _History_Forward, http://222.army.mil/women (Retrieved May 9, 2010).

Our taxes support a city of federal government workers in our nation's capitol Washington, D.C. and throughout the world. Our taxes support every agency from: the Department of State, to the Federal Bureau of Investigation; to the very institution that collects such taxes itself, the Internal Revenue Service.

Our taxes support the Army, Navy, Air Force, Marines, Coast Guard and National Guard. Moreover, our taxes support the President himself. Although our President's salary is $400,000 per year, with a $50,000.00 expense account,[66] let's not forget the fringe benefits:

1. Chief Commander of the most powerful soldier army in the world
2. Air Force One
3. Gated community mansion in the heart of the most prime real estate communities in Washington, D.C.
4. Personnel chefs, maids, butlers and other attendants.
5. Bodyguards does not accurately describe the Secret Service Agency. *If they don't care about their own lives, you know they don't care about yours.*

The President of the United States is the undisputed ruler of the world and our taxes support him, his attendants, and all of the aforementioned accoutrements that accompany this elected position. Note: Although there are some who will argue that a President is not a King, I would submit that it depends on the situation. I invite anyone to currently name a King that is more powerful than the President of these United States.

Ironically, the Bible reflects that the King will **take** a tenth and use it for his attendants while turning you into slaves.[67] *Isn't it interesting how much the word "take" is synonymous with the word "seize."*

Well, I guess the story is sgraight.[68]" Yet, in spite of all of these

---

66   Presidential Pay and Compensation, About.com US Government Info. http://usgovinfo.about. com/od/thepresidentaland cabinet/a/presidentialpay.htm. (Retrieved April 6, 2010).
67   I Samuel 8:17.
68   "straight"

challenges; in spite of God being the Omega and the Alpha; in spite of God being able to snatch victory out of the jaws of defeat; in spite of God being our sole provider for substance, joy and security, the people still insisted on having a King.

"No!" they said. "We want a king over us.[69] Then we will be like all the other nations, with a king to lead us and to go out before us and fight our battles."[70]

When Samuel heard these words, he repeated them to the LORD.[71] The LORD answered; "Listen to them and give them a king."[72] I submit that this was the genesis of the "Original Gangsta," a.k.a. "The IRS."

As we've be saying in the country, *"no need in closing the barn door after the cows have wandered off."* I think history will reflect how we really flunked the Judge versus King thing. *Why would we want to be like everybody else anyway?*

It appears in the absence of a direct intervention from God, we're stuck with the King's language, rules, and tax system. Now, God's law is superseded by Man's law.

Although we are left with what appears to be insurmountable circumstances, God always provides a way out. The Bible does not discourage Christians from implementing proactive tax strategies, as long as we play by the rules. Our first step is to embrace our new mantra: 'Render Unto Caesar that which is Caesar's But Nothing More.'

"But Nothing More" is merely playing by the rules, i.e., not only taking advantage of every deduction, but also creating deductions and placing ourselves in the best tax position possible. Yet, some have considered our approach somewhat revolutionary and I couldn't disagree more.

---

69   I Samuel 8:19 NRS
70   I Samuel 8:20 NRS
71   *Id.* at 8:21.
72   *Id.* at 8:22.

Uncle Sam is entitled to his share of taxes and I shudder to think what it would be like if we didn't pay taxes. I also believe we are only required to pay our legal share and the Government is accountable for every penny it collects.

No, my friends, this is not revolutionary thinking. A revolution is a "radical and pervasive change in society and the social structure, especially, one made suddenly and often accompanied by violence."[73] The true revolutionaries are those who choose not to pay any taxes. The true revolutionaries harmonically bellow the infamous battle cry:

"Why should we render unto Caesar when paying taxes is unconstitutional?

73 www.dictionary.com.http://dictionary.reference.com/brose/revolution (Retrieved October 2, 2009).

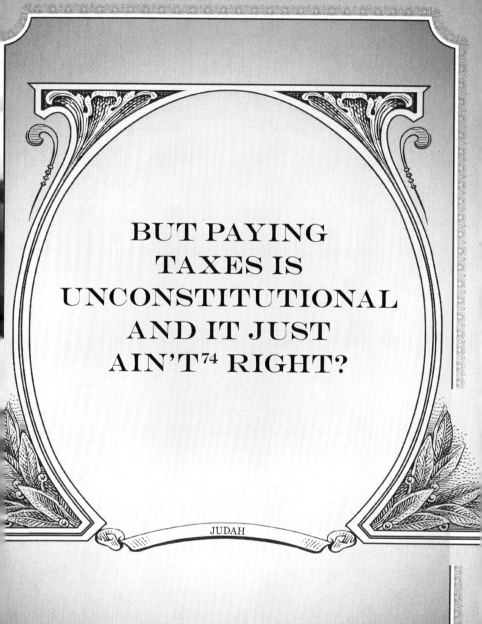

BUT PAYING
TAXES IS
UNCONSTITUTIONAL
AND IT JUST
AIN'T[74] RIGHT?

JUDAH

CHAPTER THREE

Render Unto Caesar, Yeah, Yeah, Yeah, . . . Right . . . Whatever! Why should we render unto Caesar when paying taxes is unconstitutional?

Many times I am approached by individuals who have a "quick tax question." It is so amazing how they can analyze one of the most sinister forms of law; calculate its complexity; and determine that the resolve is regulated in a relatively short period of time. Simply amazing!

Well, last Christmas while attending a party, a gentleman approached me and in an obnoxious and challenging voice said, *"You're a big shot Tax Attorney, I defy you to find in the Constitution where the US Government has the right to tax its citizens."* I'm not the kind to back down from a good fight, especially if the odds are in my favor.

I kindly asked the host if I could utilize his computer and I googled "Tax and Constitution." What do you know? The very first hit was the Sixteenth Amendment. I carefully read the Sixteenth Amendment and awaited a response.

> **Congress shall have power to lay and collect taxes on incomes, from whatever source derived, without apportionment among the several states, and without regard to any census or enumeration.** [75]

With a beaming smile over his face, the gentlemen unbelievably, loudly, abruptly and proudly professed *"I haven't paid taxes in over four (4) years and I don't give a good cat kitty what the law says."* After the crowd dispersed, I quietly pulled him aside and asked him to consider keeping that little secret to himself. The IRS has eyes and ears everywhere.

If I had the time and perhaps in a different environment, I would have told him the story about this guy named Cheek. [76] Mr. Cheek was a law

---

75   The 16th Amendment to the US Constitution Income Taxation, By Congress, Mar 17, 2006 11:32 (internet). The sixteenth amendment, March 15, 1913, Ratified Amendments 1795-1992; General Records of the United States Government; Record Group 11, National Archives..

76   *Cheek v. United States*, 498 U.S. 192 (1991).

abiding citizen.[77] He always timely filed and paid his taxes. One day, while coming home, he received a flyer advertising a seminar on the "constitutionality of taxes and how they could be avoided."[78] Mr. Cheek attended the seminar and was convinced this was the way to go.

Since, Mr. Cheek was a very smart man, he studied to show himself approved. Mr. Cheek determined that taxes were unconstitutional and much like our friend at the Christmas party, he openly and loudly professed: "Not only do I not intend to file any tax returns, I have no intention of paying them either."

Well, the IRS heard about Mr. Cheek's bravado and decided to pay him a little visit. After the IRS' examination, Mr. Cheek refused to adhere to their rules; important papers were filed with various courts; and eventually, he ended up in the United States Supreme Court (The Big Kahuna). Let me repeat, United States Supreme Court . . . *That is, "it don't be getting"*[79] *any higher.* If you don't like how they rule, you must petition Congress to promulgate a new law. *They Bad! They Real Bad!*

Much to Mr. Cheek's surprise, but not mine, the Supreme Court upheld the constitutionality of taxes. Most importantly, the Big Kahuna held that even Mr. Cheek's "good faith belief" that taxes were unconstitutional was not a defense to "willfully" not adhering to the law.[80]

Mr. Cheek's "good faith belief" argument actually backfired. The Court stated: "Planning not to file tax returns and avoid prosecution using a 'good faith belief,' is kind of like planning to kill someone using a claim of 'self-defense.' If you've planned in advance, then it shouldn't work."[81]

As you can patently see, people argue about taxes all the time and how they shouldn't have to pay them:
They use the Fifth Amendment – right against self-incrimination, The

---

77   The facts were enhanced to provide greater entertainment for the reader.
78   Facts are embellished to entertain the reader.
79   "doesn't get"
80   Tax Avoidance & Tax Evasion, Wikipedia, the Free encyclopedia, p. 10. (http://en.wikipedia.org/wiki/Tax_evasion (Retrieved 5.21.2009).
81   *Id.* (Citing Daniel B. Evans. *The Tax Protester FAQ;* downloaded 24 April 2007).

Takings Clause or the right that no person shall be "deprived of life, liberty, or property, without due process of law."[82]

They even use the Thirteenth Amendment – involuntary servitude.[83] *Isn't the Thirteenth Amendment the law that abolished slavery?*

"Involuntary Servitude? Wait a minute, I resemble that remark. Being an African American male, I can emphatically state that if anyone thinks paying taxes is involuntary servitude, then they're grossly off the mark.

Try pickin[84] cotton on a hot, humid Georgia day on a meal of pig feet and corn bread. I guarantee you, by the end of the day, you'll be begging to pay taxes, including interest and penalties.[85]

People have argued they shouldn't pay taxes, because of the Fourteenth Amendment.[86] That is, Americans are citizens of the individual states and not citizens of the United States.[87]

Some have even argued that because the federal income tax is progressive, (the more you make, the more they take) the discriminations and inequalities created by the tax should render the tax system unconstitutional.[88]

Trust me! All of these arguments have failed. You can't beat the system. I've worked for the IRS. I know!

But, maybe you can win by working within the system? (See "Get Your Mind Right"). However, I can guarantee you "bum rushing[89]" the IRS is

---

82   Tax Protestor Constitutional Arguments, Wikipedia, The Free Encyclopedia, http://en.wikipedia. org/wicki/Tax_protester_constitutional_arguments. (Retrieved 5.21.09).

83   *Id.*

84   "picking"

85   Not that I've actually ever picked cotton. But as mentioned earlier, I have been a roofer during a blistering Atlanta summer and I can imagine that it ain't no fun picking cotton.

86   Tax Protester, *Supra* cited at Footnote 82.

87   *Id.*

88   *Id.*

89   (Bum Rush: The use of excessive and overpowering force. Usually referred to a group of people forcibly entering a door of a popular event such as: a theatre, concert, or even a house party, in the absence of remuneration). *See* "Genesis." I use to be a bad boy (Emphasis on "use to").

out of the question.

When fighting the IRS you must know the law and simultaneously use a little finesse. Any other tactic just ain't[90] prudent.

When my good friend at the Christmas party dared me, he was unknowingly asking me to discuss the difference between tax evasion and tax avoidance. According to the former British Chancellor of the Exchequer Denis Healy, the difference between tax avoidance and tax evasion is the thickness of a prison wall.[91]

TAX AVOIDANCE VS. TAX EVASION
Tax Avoidance

Tax avoidance is the legal utilization of the tax regime to one's own advantage, in order to reduce the amount of tax that is payable by means that are within the law.[92] *"I don't have any idea what you just said but, whoo wee, Jeffro, you shoo do talk purrty." "Uncle Jed, I got me a first grade edumacation.[93] "*

Well, let's break it down. The focus points are "legal utilization" and "within the law." I repeat and emphasize: **"legal utilization"** and **"within the law."** Hopefully, the need to reiterate a third time is unnecessary; but, for those who still don't understand, **"by any *legal* means necessary."** The question is "how do we do this?" (See "Get Your Mind Right," *infra*).

---

90 "isn't"
91 Tax Protestor at Wikipedia, *Supra* cited at Footnote 82.
92 Tax Avoidance at Wikipedia, *Supra* cited at Footnote 80.
93 The Beverly Hillbillies is an American situation comedy originally broadcast for nine (9) seasons on CBS from 1962 to 1971. The series is about a poor backwoods family transplanted to Beverly Hills, CA. Created by Paul Henning. *See* (http://wikipedia.org/wiki/The_Beverly_Hillbillies) (Retrieved 07.01.120.

While a tax protestor[94] openly attempts to evade tax, a smart taxpayer avoids tax. Tax avoiders not only exploit loopholes in the law; they create them.

How can we create them? Simple, lobby our Congresspersons for a change in the law. But let's keep it real. Since this is America, if most of us don't have the loot or a collective force, then our lobbying efforts are truly in vain.

I remember attending the thirtieth year celebration of Dr. Martin Luther King Jr.'s "I Have A Dream" speech and seeing a man of lighter hue[95] wearing a t-shirt that said: "Don't Whine . . . Organize!" Maybe if we decide to organize our individual voices and create a collective force, then maybe our wants will be heard and satisfied, especially since we have the backing of the Big Kahuna. That's right, even the United States Supreme Court has held that every individual has a legal right to avoid taxes by any legal means.[96]

So you see my friends, we have the Big Kahuna's blessings to avoid tax. Tax avoidance activities can include: renouncing one's residence or citizenship;[97] creating legal entities to reduce tax liabilities;[98] and any other creative legal vehicle or combination therein.[99]

Tax Evasion

To paraphrase the munchkin guarding the doors to the emerald palace in the Wizard of Oz: *"Tax evasion is a horse of a completely different*

---

94 Tax Avoidance at Wikipedia, *Supra* at Footnote 80. Cf. Tax resistor. A Tax Resistor declares that he is refusing to pay a tax for conscientious reasons. The Government interprets these actions as one who does not want to support the government or some of its activities. Tax resistors typically do not take the position that the tax laws are themselves illegal (or don't apply to them). As tax protestors, they are interested in not paying for the particular government policies that they oppose.

95 Caucasian Male.

96 *See* Gregory v. Helvering, Commissioner of Internal Revenue (293 U.S. 465, 55 S. Ct. 266)(1935).

97 *See* Tax Avoidance, *Supra* cited at Footnote 80.

98 *Id.*

99 *See* "Get Your Mind Right"

color[100] *and that color could be the black and grey walls of a prison
cell."*

Tax evasion is the general term for efforts by individuals, firms, trusts
and other entities to evade taxes by *illegal* means.[101] Tax evasion usually
reeks of illegality with a hint of shadiness.

Most tax evaders endure painstaking calculations to deliberately feign
or mask the true state of their transactions in order to reduce their tax
liability.[102] Tax evasion is frequently seen in dishonest tax reporting;
such as declaring less income, profits or gains than actually earned; or
overstating deductions.[103] *Sound familiar?*

In 2007, the IRS estimated that Americans owed three hundred and
fifty-four billion dollars ($345,000,000.000.00) more than they actually
paid.[104] How many of us could have used a slice of that $345 billion
pizza? According to statistics, that's about 14% of the reserves for the
2007 fiscal year.[105]

Wait a minute, I think we missed it again. If $345 billion dollars is 14%
of the federal reserve, then the total federal reserve is . . . just a second,
let me do the math.

Sorry it took so long. I had to go and get another calculator that could
accommodate quadrillions. If $345 billion is 14% of the total 2007 tax
year reserves, then the total reserves was two quadrillions, four hundred
and fifteen trillion dollars ($2,415,000,000,000,000). *Wow! That's why
our Government can give away millions of dollars and it ain't no*[106] *big
deal.*

---

100   Wizard of Oz, Directed by Victor Fleming (Based on 1900 Children's novel "The Wonderful
Wizard of Oz" by L. Frank Baum. Release Date: August 15, 1939.
101   Tax Avoidance at Wikipedia, *Supra* cited at Footnote 80.
102   *Id.*
103   *Id.*
104   *Id.*
105   *Id.*
106   "isn't any"

Tax evasion is a crime in almost all countries and the guilty parties are subject to fines and/or imprisonment.[107] In China, the tax evasion punishment can lead to the death penalty.[108] *Thank God for America. At least we ain't*[109] *there yet.*

Ever wonder why the spy movies always speak of moving money to a Swiss Bank Account? In Switzerland, many acts that would amount to criminal tax evasion in other countries are treated as civil matters.[110] Even dishonestly misreporting income on a tax return is not necessarily considered a crime.[111] *Wow, what a county. Oleta ... hoo.*

But let's not get carried away. If you're skiing on the Swiss Alps and decide to deliberately falsify records, then civil penalties may apply and you may even go to jail.[112] So, although the differences between Switzerland and other countries are significant, some limitations still exist.[113]

In the good ole USA, tax evasion is:

> Any person who willfully attempts, in any manner to evade or defeat any tax imposed by this title or the payment thereof shall in addition to other penalties provided by law, be guilty of a felony and, upon conviction shall be fined not more than one hundred thousand dollars ($100,000.00) (five hundred thousand dollars ($500,000.00) in the case of a corporation), or imprisonment not more than five (5) years, or both, together with the costs of prosecution.[114]

---

107 *See* Tax Avoidance, *Supra* cited at Footnote 80.

108 *Id.*

109 "are not"

110 *See* Tax Avoidance, *Supra* cited at Footnote 80.

111 *Id.*

112 *Id.*

113 *Id.* Most authorities consider the severity of intent in determining the degree of punishment. Normally, the higher the amount evaded, the higher the degree of punishment.

114 26 U.S.C. 7201

Let's all do the James Brown[115] (aka God Father of Soul) camel walk and "break it down:"

Any Person:

Any person can include: me, you, and your grandmamma too; a corporation, partnership, limited liability company, and any individual and collective derivative that one can create therein. Let me put it this way, if the IRS is pushed, it will even tax the imaginary friend seen by many kids, and some adults. I can see it now: *"You see your honor, it wasn't me, but it was my imaginary friend named, ummm, 'Roscoe,' yeah that's his name Roscoe."*

Suffice to say that, if you can think of it, the IRS will find a way to tax it. My recommendation is not to fight this one. I don't think you'll win.

Any Tax:

I dare say at least ninety percent (90%) of all taxpayers are unaware of the taxes created by Congress and collected by the IRS. Let's see, there's:

- Income Taxes (most of us know this one)
- Estate & Gift Taxes
- Corporate Taxes
- Subchapter S Corporate Taxes
- Property Taxes
- Partnership Taxes
- International Taxes
- Employee Plans Taxes
- Just to name a few.

---

115   James Joseph Brown (May 3, 1933 – December 25, 2006) was an American singer, songwriter, musician, and recording artist. He is the originator of funk music and is a major figure of 20th century popular music and dance. http://en.wikipedia.org/wiki/James_brown (Retrieved February 21, 2012).

There's even a tax for nonprofits. *"I thought that nonprofits were exempt from federal income taxes."*

Yeah, they are, but tax-exempt organizations are also subject to Unrelated Business Income Taxes, Self-Employment Taxes (Social Security Taxes and Medicare), and other State and Local Taxes given the proper circumstances.

Again, this is part of the challenge. Because our tax system is so complicatedly broad, wide and deep, it is extremely challenging to fight. And just think, the IRS is collecting paper from all of these transactions. Mo' Money, Mo' Money, Mo' *Money.* [116]

In any manner:

I don't care what "had happened."[117] *"Any manner" means "any manner."* Moving funds from one account to another is, under most circumstances, a perfectly legal and sometimes sound financial decision. However, the IRS will interpret such actions as a willful attempt to evade taxes and subject you to a lot of ugly things mentioned later in the statute.[118]

In addition to other penalties provided by law:

I don't give a good kitty[119] about how you have already been found guilty somewhere else; time concurrently served with the State or other international authorities; or anything else. *"Boy, you in my house now." (Written in a good ole boy southern accent).*

Be guilty of a felony and upon conviction shall be fined not more than

---

116 The Wayans Brothers Show. Created by Shawn Wayans, Marlon Wayans, Leslie Ray and David Steven Simon, Executive Producers: Billy Van Zandt & Jane Milmore (Season 1), Rick Hawkins (Season 2), Phil Kellard & Tom Moore (Seasons 3-5), Distributor: Warner Bros. Television (January 11, 1995 – May 20, 1999).

117 "happened"

118 Tax Avoidance at Wikipedia, *Supra* cited at Footnote 80.

119 "Good Kitty" is used in the most respectful terms. No disrespect intended. Used exclusively for emphasis purposes. My Father always told me not to curse because I was much more intelligent than that. I always told him that "it always felt so good as though there was a release of energy. As I got older, I discovered what he knew already . . . Father Knows Best.

one hundred thousand dollars ($100,000.00) (five hundred thousand dollars ($500,000.00) in the case of a corporation), or imprisonment not more than five (5) years, or both, together with the costs of prosecution:

Ugly Things:

1. Felony – Federal Pen. Bubba's Big Brother. *No way Hosea!*
2. Fined up to one hundred thousand dollars ($100,000.00). *I don't know about you, but that's a lot of money to me.*
3. Both – You put me in the federal pen and fine me one hundred thousand bucks ($100,000.00). *Why are you being so mean to me?*
4. Cost of Prosecution – *Let me make sure that I understand the worst case scenario. You sentence me to the federal pen; you also fine me one hundred thousand bucks ($100,000.00); and you're going to make me pay for the cost of the IRS prosecuting me, including Court fees. Didn't your Mother love you?*
5. Coos De Gras – *Let's not forget that on top of all that was mentioned, you still gotta pay the tax, including penalties and interest.*

Just writing about it runs a shiver down my spine. I was always one of those kids who would immediately change after narrowly escaping a mischievous venture gone wrong.

The sad part about it is that the IRS has the resources to attack from several fronts with all abandonment. It ain't a pretty picture and there's no way around it. Intentionally filing a false tax return is a separate crime in itself.[120]   And don't get it twisted[121], ignorance of the law is **no** excuse.[122]

According to estimates, approximately three percent (3%) of all

---

120   *See* 26 USC 7206
121   "Confused"
122   Wikipedia (Citing "Ignorantia legis neminem excusat, or "ignorance of law excuses no one.") Black's Law Dictionary, p 673 (5th ed. 1979))

taxpayers do not file tax returns.[123] The civil penalty for **willful** failure to timely **"file"** a return is generally equal to five percent (5%) of the tax on the return, **per month**, up to a maximum of 25%.[124] By contrast, the civil penalty for **willful** failure to timely **"pay"** the tax actually "shown on the return" is generally equal to one half of one percent (0.5%) due, **per month**, up to a maximum of twenty-five percent (25%).[125]

The two penalties are computed conjointly in a complex algorithm upon which we receive a certified letter containing a most intimidating bill from the IRS. It's put together absolutely beautifully. *Don't hate, learn from the game.*[126]

If you decide not to file a return, then the statute of limitations on civil actions goes on forever.[127] That is, the IRS can hunt you down to the end of time in order to seek and destroy.

For each year a taxpayer willfully fails to timely file an income tax return, the taxpayer can be sentenced to one year in prison.[128] *"Momma, there go that man again."*

Interestingly enough, if taxes "ain't" constitutional, the consequences of not filing and paying them sure do accompany some pretty stiff penalties. Hopefully our Christmas party friend will read this book or hear about it. I would hate for him to incur the true wrath of the IRS.

Actually, he's not unique in his situation. Many everyday people choose to disobey the law every day. Not only average citizens like you and me, but celebrities too. The list is endless: Sophie Loren, Wesley Snipes, Willie Nelson, Ronald Isley, and the most infamous celebrity of all time

---

123   www.enotes.com/taxes-reference/tax-evasion Referenced from: (Encyclopedia of Everyday Law. Editor Brian J. Koski, Jeffrey Wilson and Ralph G. Zerbonia. 2003.

124   *See* 26 U.S.C. §6651(a)(1)

125   *See* 26 U.S.C. §6651(a)(2)

126   Take the positive from every situation and apply it for good.

127   *See* 26 U.S.C. §6501

128   *See* 26 U.S.C. 7503

Alphonse Capone.[129] Well, celebrities may have it a little different. Hopefully, in making millions of dollars, they've hired competent accountant firms to handle their money because accountant firms don't make mistakes. Right?

When I was working at PricewaterhouseCoopers and Ernst & Young, the accountants looked down upon the legal profession and this hateration[130] was accompanied by a myriad of jokes. They would laugh all the good day long.

Then one day "Enron" popped up.[131] *What? You mean to tell me the accountants are cooking the books, i.e. lying to show a prosperous year and fortuitous future. Well, to quote Tweety Bird, that's down right despicable.*[132]

All of a sudden, the laughter was replaced by silence. If you can't trust your accountant, who can you trust?

Isn't it interesting that inevitably when celebrities are audited by the IRS, they always proclaim the same statement . . . "It was my accountant's fault. I had nothing to do with it." Though this may be true, the IRS stills hold you responsible in spite of the legal complexity. However, as we discussed earlier, there are some who "don't know" and there are others who "don't care."

Trust me; it is patently clear that it is more beneficial to play the game than evade it. Moreover, playing by the rules promotes good sleep. In other words, regardless of the situation, we must practice tax avoidance

---

129   Don't Mess With Taxes: Celebrity.
http://dontmesswithtaxes.typepad.com/dont_mess_taxes/celebrity/ (Retrieved 9.15.08).
130   The narrative form of "hating" in the colloquium sense.
131   Google Enron and see what interesting goodies come up.
132   Looney Tunes is a Warner Bros. animated cartoon series and its first official release was in the 1930s and it has become a worldwide media franchise, spawning several television series, films, comics, music albums, video games and amusement park rides. Looney Tunes' most well-known and popular cartoon characters in history, including Bugs Bunny, Daffy Duck, Tweety Bird and Porky Pig. FYI Mel Blanc was a Black Man that was known as the voices behind many of the Looney Tunes characters. From 1942 until 1969, Looney Tunes was the most popular short cartoon series in theaters, exceeding Disney and other popular competitors. *See* http://en.wikipedia.org/wiki/Looney_Tunes. (Retrieved 4.28.2012).

and *"Render Unto Caesar, That Which Is Caesar's . . . But Nothing More!*

It's always been said if we don't learn from our past, then we're bound to repeat it. History tells us of a famous gentleman who became a billionaire and refused to pay taxes. His name was Alphonse Capone. Maybe we can learn from his history. It is with great pleasure that I introduce "The Original Gangsta."

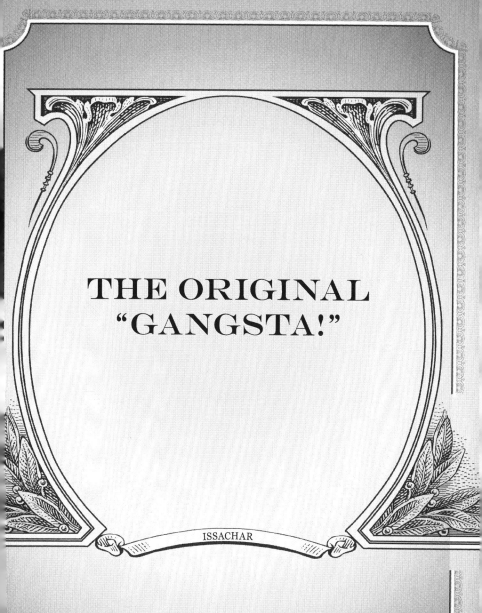

THE ORIGINAL "GANGSTA!"

ISSACHAR

CHAPTER FOUR

Only as a former "Consigliore" / "Ex-federate," with a working knowledge of the Internal Revenue Service, can I emphatically state, with the utmost amount of respect, that the IRS is the "**The Original Gangsta!**" Other than God, the IRS is the only entity that can strike fear in the hearts of men and women with the mere mention of its name.[133]

How many of us have received a letter from the IRS and our hearts began to quiver; hands shake; mouths gets dry . . . Some of us refuse to open the letter, unknowingly compounding the situation exponentially because the IRS will not be ignored!

At TaxConcepts, we serve as power of attorney for numerous individuals, corporations and partnerships. As "ex-federate," one would think that I am accustomed to receiving letters from the IRS. It's my job.

However, on some occasions, even I take a double look upon receiving batches of certified letters from the Internal Revenue Service on behalf of our clients as the postal person kindly requests a signature. This fear and respect is only seen in gangster movies.

If you ever watch the "Untouchables[134]" with Kevin Costner, ask yourself "who is the bad guy?" Both are committing murder, using unreasonable force, and each considers themselves beyond reproach. However, the IRS had unlimited sovereign resources substantiated by the U.S. Constitution to ensure that Capone showed the proper respect.

There are a plethora of books, records, movies and other media consistently naming Al Capone as the most infamous gangster from his birth on January 17 1899,[135] to current gangster history. As the most renowned gangster, Capone's life was constantly in danger.

---

133   The IRS would strike the fear into the hearts of little children, but they are too young to realize the gravity of the situation.

134   The Untouchables; Directed by Brian De Palma; Written by: Oscar Fraley (suggested by book) and Elliot Ness (suggested by book), release date 3 June '87.

135   Al Capone, Wikipedia, the Free Encyclopedia, http://en.wikipedia.org/wiki/Al_Capone) (Retrieved 9/17/09).

In spite of the IRS' unlimited resources, there was the infamous equalizer. . . the "Thompson Submachine Gun" aka:
- Tommy Gun
- Trench Sweeper
- Chicago Piano
- Chicago Typewriter and
- My all time favorite, "The Chopper.[136]"

The Chopper was favored by police and criminals alike because of its:
- Ergonomics *(No lie that's what the paper had done said)*[137]
- Compactness *(Easily transported & concealed)*.
- Large 45 ACP 1 cartridge *(It "be holding"[138] a lot of bullets)*
- High volume of automatic fire. *(I think you got this one.)*

With the invention of the "Chopper," the whole game changed. Now when rival gangs decided to hang out with each other or with the Feds, having fun was no longer "Pop. . . . . Pop. . . . .Pop" But rather "Pop, Pop, Pop, Pop, Pop, Pop, Pop x 35 more times."

Naturally, with the Chopper, murder was on the rise; rival syndicate bosses had assignation contracts on Capone's life to kill on sight; and to make matters worse, the public knew that the Federal Bureau of Investigation made Al Capone "Public Enemy Number One."[139] Yet, during this era of prohibition, the most infamous tax evasion case of all time arose. The IRS succeeded, where the FBI and crime bosses had failed.

In 1931, Al Capone (Scarface) was not convicted of violating federal prohibition, prostitution, and/or gambling, but income tax invasion.[140] That's right . . . "income tax evasion." Scarface went to the federal

---

136   American submachine gun invented by John T. Thompson in 1919.
Thompson Submachine Gun, Wikipedia, the free encyclopedia. (http:/en.wikipedia.org/wiki/Tommy_gun).
137   "said"
138   "holds"
139   *See* Al Capone, cited at Footnote 135.
140   *Id.*

penitentiary, because he did not file and pay his income taxes like every other American.

If the IRS can accomplish what the Federal Bureau of Investigation and other syndicate bosses could not, who is really the "Original Gangsta?" *Things that make you go hhhhmmmmm!*

A good friend of mine has a favorite movie called the "Wizard of Oz."[141] Most people think that the moral of the story is "there is no place like home." While this is true, there is another equally, if not greater, underlying theme.

My friend taught me that the most important lesson of the movie is

Pay Attention To The Man Behind The Curtain

For those who don't know, this is the scene when Toto (the dog) reveals that the enormous fire spitting, directive giving, fear driving, floating human head is merely an image created by a mortal hiding behind a curtain, manipulating multiple levels and levers. Therefore, the real lesson is: when confronted with interesting and challenging situations, ***"Pay Attention To The Man Behind The Curtain."***

After working almost ten (10) years with the Internal Revenue Service, I know the real deal behind the curtain. Comparing the IRS to the Mafia, Costra Nostra, or the Syndicate is something that most Americans have done for generations. And if you observe carefully, each organizations operate on similar principles. The remainder of this chapter is dedicated to these principles.

Numero Uno: It's All About "Respect"

News Flash! It wasn't just income tax evasion that resulted in the conviction of Al Capone, it was "DISRESPECT." Respect is always the lynchpin principle of any gangster movie from the Godfather to

---

141   Wizard of Oz Directed, *Supra* cited at Footnote 100.

Scarface. Disrespect is not tolerated and if you're lucky, you get a warning before you're whacked.

The IRS could not allow Scarface to blatantly disrespect it by not paying his fair share. Capone failed to report one million, fifty-five thousand, three hundred and seventy-five dollars and five cents (($1,055,375.05) of taxable income.[142] WOW!

For those of us who have lived long enough, we all know brilliant people who took the wrong path. *Capone was one of those people.* Capone brilliantly managed a million dollar empire exclusively with cash. Yet, in spite of his massive fortune, Capone disrespected the Godfather by not paying his fair share.

The IRS will not permit a million dollars to slip through its "collective little hands." You must pay the Godfather the proper respect by providing a portion of your earnings for the protection he provides. The rule is simple - pay the Godfather the proper respect or suffer the consequences. If the Internal Revnue Service permits one individual to forgo paying taxes, then the floodgate will burst for everyone. *"We must make an example of Scarface!"*

Only a Made Man Can Whack Another Made Man.

In 1929, *Tony* (written in an Italian Accent) received the order to whack Al Capone. On this date, the Internal Revenue Bureau[143] assigned Revenue Agents W.C. Hodgins, Jacque L. Westrich and H.N. Clagett (collectively referred to as *"Tony"*) the monumental task of bringing down Public Enemy No. 1, Al Capone.[144]

Recently released documents[145] show how *Tony* struggled to connect Capone's income to sources such as prostitution, gambling or

---

142 IRS Released Files From Case Against "hoodlum" Capone. *See* The Boston Globe, Boston.com (http://www.boston.com/news/nation/washington/articles/2008/03/01/irs_releases_files_from...) Retrieved (9.17.09). Note: The IRS always knows down to the penny of every liability owned.
143 *Id.* The IRS was initially called the Internal Revenue Bureau.
144 *Id.*
145 www.IRS.gov Search Al Capone Documents

bootlegging during the Prohibition Era, all while contemporaneously avoiding assassination. *"Assassination?"*

Yes, assassination. Al Capone had amassed a, multi-million dollar empire and killing federal agents and rival gang members was all in a day's work. Capone could solicit a multi-million dollar murder contract, not be "out of pocket[146], and still half a line of henchmen stretched around the block two times.

How could the IRS accomplish what everyone else could not? Al Capone never had a bank account and only on one occasion, could it be found where he ever endorsed a check.[147] Let me repeat that, he never had a bank account. Capone took operating a business on a *"cash basis"* to a whole nother level."[148]

Tony was unable to find where "Capone was stashing the loot."[149] Since Capone only transacted in cash, *Tony* was systematically reduced to finding a snitch and making him squeal like a pig.

Aha, the bookkeeper! Since Capone only carried cash, the only nexus to the billion dollars was the bookkeeper.

"Why keep books if you're engaging in illegal activities?" At Capone's level, prostitution, gambling and drugs were a highly lucrative and sophisticated business. You can compromise the tender, be it cash, securities, or other financial vehicles. But, there is no substitute for "keeping the books." You gotta know the state of your affairs.

If you don't know where you are and where you've been, the chances of discovering where you're going is improbable. Even the Bible states to know the "state of your assets."[150]

---

146   Would not incur a substantial loss to the point that business is strained, terminated.
147   Boston Globe, *Supra* cited at Footnote 142.
148   Inventing a new paradigm.
149   Recording the transactions pursuant to Generally Accepted Accounting Principles (GAAP).
150   Proverbs 27:23 -24. Be thou diligent to know the state of thy flocks, and look well to thy herds. For riches are not for ever and doth the crown endure to every generation? (Note: "look" is interpreted as "attend to." (King James Version) Thomas Nelson Publishers.

Capone operated his business more efficiently than any legal business could hope. Come to think of it, operating a multi-million dollar business during the late 1920's had to place Capone in the top ten (10) businesses. Trust me, Scarface knew the "state of his assets" and "the bookkeeper was the key." Note: *Be kind to your bookkeeper and pay them their just worth plus. He or she could save your life.*

I can imagine that, if anyone deserved any sympathy, it's the bookkeeper. He was stuck between the proverbial rock and hard place.[151]

On one end of the spectrum, there was Scarface, a criminal known for his viciousness, killing efficiency, and ability to evade the law. Whereas, on the other end, there was the Federal Bureau of Investigation and the Internal Revenue Service. *"What to do? What to do?"*

Tony was successful in reaching the bookkeeper. Query: What could the IRS possibly say or do to make Capone's Bookkeeper snitch against a vicious killer. *All together now. . . hhmmmm!*

Records reflect that *Tony* went to such extreme measures as hiding the bookkeeper in South America[152] to minimize the opportunity of any unlucky accident befalling him like getting shot in the head by a police officer or hanging himself in his jail cell or being struck by lightning.[153] *You get the picture.*

Although Capone avoided process of service, bribed juries, murdered witnesses, and committed violent attacks on federal agents, he was convicted of five counts of income tax evasion and one sentence of failing to file a tax return.[154] Al Capone went to jail for not paying three hundred and eighty-three thousand, seven hundred and five dollars and

---

151 Any evidence secured had to be developed through the testimony of associates or others which, through fear of personal injury, or loyalty was most difficult to obtain Boston Globe, *Supra* cited at Footnote 142.

152 *Id.*

153 "The Godfather," Directed by Francis Ford Coppola. Screenplay by Mario Puzo and Francis Ford Coppola. Based on Mario Puzo's Novel "The Godfather." Produced by Albert S. Ruddy (1972) Paramount Pictures. All Rights Reserved.

154 Al Capone, Wikipedia, *Supra* cited at Footnote 135.

twenty-one cents ($383,705.21) in taxes and penalties. [155]

Capone was sentenced to eleven (11) years in prison. [156] He served time in the Atlanta Federal Penitentiary; eventually transferred to Alcatraz. [157] and was released for good behavior after six (6) years of time. Alphonse Capone died in 1947. [158]

Thus, the Internal Revenue of Service succeeded, where the FBI and other syndicate bosses had failed. Why? *Because only a Made Man Can Whack a Made Man!*

"Give the Godfather his Respect. Timely File Your Tax Return. Pay the Godfather his Proper Portion."

Al Capone lost his multi-million dollar empire because he did not file his income tax returns and pay the appropriate taxes. Sure, I know what you're thinking. If Capone reports income from his prostitution, gambling, and bootlegging activities, then the return would be an admission of guilt and the FBI could convict him for violating prohibition laws.

Remember, "Pay Attention to the Man Behind the Curtain." In this case, keep your eye on the "Cleaner," because he (or she) makes the dirty activities come out clean as Colorado snow on a clear spring day on the slopes of Vale. *Yeah Man!*

The "Cleaner" is responsible for transforming broken laws into taxable corporate activities. In hindsight, if a "Made Man" approached Capone with the scenario of filing his annual return and paying three hundred and eighty-three thousand, seven hundred and fifty-one dollars and twenty one cents ($383,751.21) in taxes and penalties in exchange for keeping his billion dollar empire, he would timely file and pay the taxes with footnotes, binders, a coke and a smile. [159]

---

155 Boston, *Supra* cited at Footnote 142.
156 Al Capone, Wikipedia, *Supra* cited at Footnote 135.
157 *Id.*
158 *Id.*
159 Coke trademark.

Moreover, filing your taxes binds the IRS to confidentiality, because of the Freedom Information Act (FIA).[160] Unfortunately, we live in an era where "identity theft" is a reality and as we tell our clients, a good tax person knows more about you than your Pastor, Minister, Rabbi, Monk, etc. They know:

- Your Social Security Number
- Where you live
- If you're married
- How many kids you have
- If you own or rent a home
- How much you give to your religious organization
- Where you're employed
- What kind of investments are held in your portfolio
- Etc. Etc. Etc.

Because of the FIA, there is restricted access to an individual's tax return or other tax-related information. Query: *If the FIA prohibits the IRS from releasing financial and tax information, how is it that we were able to obtain Capone's gross revenue, assessed tax liabilities, and other private information?*

Jonathan Elg, author of "Get Capone," made the request from the IRS.[161] Elg said that he was "casting a wide net" and was "shocked" that the IRS complied."[162] Note: Don't be afraid to ask. *All they can say is "hell no!"*

---

160 *See* Boston, *Supra* cited at Footnote 142.
161 *Id.*
162 *Id.*

In 1989, the United States Court of Appeals for the Fifth Circuit said "Hell No!"[163] James Calder, a professor at the University of Texas in San Antonio, made the same request and was emphatically denied.[164] The IRS refused to provide access to Capone's records, and the Courts agreed that Calder had no right to access such records pursuant to the Constitution or any other federal laws.[165]

During the time, Calder was researching a book, implicating President Hoover as the "man behind the curtain."[166] That is, Mr. Hoover was responsible for orchestrating the Capone investigation.[167]

"The whole thing is irritating the hell out of me, frankly" Calder said of the IRS decision to release the records.[168] Elg replied by stating that the decision probably occurred because "there are lawyers at the IRS taking a different perspective."[169]

Elg added that the agency probably considers the release of the Capone records as good publicity; that is, the Capone case, "is one of the few things connected to the IRS that people have a warm and fuzzy feeling about.[170]

"IRS" and *"warm and fuzzy"* in the same sentence is the classical example of an oxymoron. They just don't go together.

The only things "warm and fuzzy" about the IRS are:

1. The fact that they don't contact you (or as I've heard some client's say *"just leave me lone"*).
2. Receiving a refund because of an unexpected error in your favor. *Yeah right, how often does this happen?*
3. Receiving a letter stating that your organization is exempt from

---

163 *Id.*
164 *Id.*
165 *Id.*
166 *Id.*
167 *Id.*
168 *Id.*
169 *Id.*
170 *Id.*

federal income taxes pursuant to Internal Revenue Code §501(c)(3).

Even the IRS stated releasing Capone's records was highly unusual because of the FIA.[171] However, the Service stated that it decided to make the memos pubic, because Capone never filed a tax return.[172]

"Dried Bull Hockey with dead horse flies!" The IRS ultimately released the memos, because it wanted to. The IRS bows down only to the United States Supreme Court (a.k.a. "The Big Kahuna"), and that's it. My federate' instincts tell me that the memos were released to remind the public of its power and market its new theme - "We got Al Capone. We can get you too."

Opps, I almost missed it. Did you say that the Original Gangsta made Capone's revenue information available to the general public, because he did not properly file a tax return? That's right, "Pay Attention to the Man Behind the Curtain."

If you don't file a tax return, then it appears as though the Original Gangsta has the right to release all of your private financial information to anyone who submits a request. This precedent encourages filing your income tax returns, because, in the alternative, "all of your business is in the streets." Note: At one time, the IRS could make tax returns available to the general public. (*See* "The Big Hustle").

Moral of the Story: "Timely File And Pay Your Income Taxes." By the way, remember our friend Capone and his disrespectful ways.

After convicting Capone and sending him to the federal penitentiary, the IRS seized all of his accounts. That's right, took the money anyway.[173] All of it! *If that ain't gangsta, I don't know what is.*

I strongly encourage you to give the Godfather his proper respect and

---

171 *Id.*

172 *Id.*

173 Query: By the way, what did the Internal Revenue of Bureau do with all of that money?

pay him his proper portion. (*See* Render Unto Caesar . . . But Nothing More.) If the Original Gangsta can bring down the infamous Scarface, he can bring you down, too!

THE WORLD IS FILLED WITH "PIMPS & HUSTLERS"

EPHRAIM

CHAPTER FIVE

I find it difficult to believe that our forefathers could conceive that their actions would create the most complicated tax system in the world. Today, our tax system is so unnecessarily complex it's unbelievable.

The Internal Revenue Code is further explained by the Treasury Regulations, which are further explained by Revenue Rulings and Procedures, which may be modified by Court Cases, and on and on. *What are they trying to hide?*

According to the Original Gangsta, we have a voluntary tax system. That is, the government relies on individual citizens to: report their income freely and voluntarily; calculate their tax liability correctly; and file a tax return on a timely basis."[174]

Most people, self included, don't really get the "voluntary" part. Let's see:

- the Government (Feds and State) takes our money from each paycheck;
- if we don't withhold enough during the year, then we're penalized;
- if our return yields a tax liability and we don't submit full payment on April 15th, then our balance is subject to interest from April 16th until the debt is satisfied;
- if we don't satisfy the balance in a reasonable amount of time, the Original Gangsta may assess additional penalties; and
- if we give too much, then we must calculate, complete and submit a designated Form to get the money that we're owed. And did I mention that we receive our money in the absence of any interest?

This seems like a no-win situation. By the way and excuse me, but somehow I missed the *"voluntary"* part.

I don't understand how a system can purport to be voluntary when the Original Gangsta has the right to randomly conduct audits and if need be, bring in the heavy and shut down shop to get the money that we *"voluntarily"* owe?

---

174   *See* USC 26 IRC 6072(a).

"Don't hate the player, learn from the game."[175] This tax thing sounds like one of the best games in town. The real question is, *"How do I get in on the game?"*

In all this tax madness, there are individuals, like our friend at the Christmas party, who emphatically proclaim, *"taxes are unconstitutional and damn it, I'm not going to pay them."* These constitutional arguments have failed for decades. *See* But Paying Taxes Is Unconstitutional . . .

The critical thinker asks, *"How do I get in on the game?"* While one dude is thinking, "taxes are illegal and I must profess it to the world," there are others who are "straight up "pimpin"[176] the tax law system right before our very eyes.

At the Internal Revenue Service, PricewaterhouseCoopers, and Ernst & Young, I worked with sophisticated taxes. Nice and clean. Probably best described as white collar tax or crime depending on whether the glass is half empty or half full and the creativity of your hopefully competent counsel.

I was completely oblivious as to how dirty the personal income tax game is. I had absolutely no clue. It's worse than any drug or pimp show that you've ever seen.

The game begins by convincing low-income individuals that a refund is a good thing. (*See* Proverbial Question). Then, you sell them on the concept it's better to have it now, so you can satisfy some outstanding debts, buy a new shiny television set, or just have a little extra money in your pocket to party with.

Pimp Daddy: "Hey man, come here for a minute. Check this deal out. I can get you one thousand dollars ($1,000.00) within twenty-four (24) hours."

---

175   Don't succumb to discouragement, jealousy or resentment, because you see them doing spiritually, financially, or emotionally well. Learn the inside track and proactively maximize it to your advantage. Compliments of Lauren Z. Smith, Esq.
176   Take an unfair advantage of those who don't know any differently.

Note: He doesn't tell you that there are hidden loan fees. But is it really hidden if it's hiding on the paper? **Read People Read.** And if you don't understand, say "I don't understand." The first step to recovery is recognition.

Pimp Daddy: "*Let me do your taxes today and we can put some paper in your pocket tomorrow. How does that sound?*"

John: "Tomorrow, really, yeah that sounds good. I was checking out this 42" high definition flat screen that would look fit perfectly in my apartment."

Pimp Daddy does your taxes lickity split like he promised, you got cheese[177] in your pocket the very next day. In the back of your mind, you're thinking, "*that Pimp Daddy is a really nice guy. I must recommend him to all of my friends. I got a good deal.*" Little do you know, but you just got suckered!

When Pimp Daddy electronically files your taxes you don't receive a refund, you received a Refund Anticipation Loan ("RAL"). RALS are actually more costly than beneficial.

Last year, 8.67 million low income taxpayers spent nine hundred million ($900,000,000.00) in loan fees.[178] *Nine hundred million - hell you might as well say one billion ($1,000,000,000).*

This is how the hustle works. The "Tax Preparer" is the "Pimp" and the "Bank" is the "Hustler." The Pimp and the Hustler are obviously in on the deal and working hand-in-hand. The Pimp obtains a loan from a local Hustler based on the expected refund of the tax return. This service, however, is not provided for free. *Are you kidding me?*

---

177   "money"

178   The Tax Refund Hustle, The Atlanta Voice, February 6-12, 2009, Volume No. 44 issue No. 28, Page 1&14 (citing Jean Ann Fox, Director of Financial Services at the Consumer Federation of America).

The Pimp and the Hustler inflate their individual service fees and they've taken their paper from your RAL right off the top. That is, before receiving "*your*" money, they've already been "pazzaid"[179] from the loan that you're legally obligated to repay.

The RAL fees can range from forty percent (40%) to one hundred and seventy-eight percent (178%). Most people pay an average of seventy-seven percent (77%) annual interest against their own money.[180] Some Pimps charge an additional twenty dollars ($20.00) to forty-five dollars ($45.00) on top of these percentages.[181] You do the math. Heard this before: Mo' *money, Mo' Money, Mo' Money!*[182]

"*I don't believe you. Who are these people that are allegedly pimping me?*" You know them: Jackson Hewitt, H&R Block, Liberty Tax Service and any other tax preparer who engages in such usury activities. I've even seen a small time pimp in a gas station offering rapid refunds. True!

Realistically, these hustlers are no different than other pimps or drug pushers who rape and pillage our communities. They make their money off the disadvantaged and don't restore the communities with the loot they take.

If it were about anything other than paper/cheese,[183] then they would teach the people how to save and invest their RALs. *Why not? Couldn't hurt.*

Well maybe it could. With applied knowledge comes power, enlightenment and responsibility. When one spark is ignited and you realize you're getting pimped, there is a duty to enlighten others.

Pimp Daddy: "Are you kidding me? We can't have that! Somebody
shut this guy up; he's ruining it for everybody. Don't
you realize we have mortgage payments for our vacation

---

179 "Paid"
180 *See* The Tax Refund Hustle, *Supra* cited at Footnote 178.
181 *Id.* Citing H&R Block according to the National Consumer Law Center.
182 *See* The Wayans Brothers, *Supra* cited at Footnote 116.
183 "money"

homes in Aruba and Dubai? What about our limousine driver's family? Are we supposed to put our chauffeurs on the streets? I'm helping to support his family and in turn the American economy."

The game is designed to exploit low-income individuals. RALs are promoted in low-income communities in order to socio-economically manipulate those who need a refund check faster.

At one time, I thought it was hidden racism. But is it really racism when it's in "black & white" and no one is forcing you to submit your John Hancock? As a good friend of mine always says: *"Everything ain't the White Man's fault. He's responsible for a lot, but not everything."*

Although the ghettos are primarily occupied by African Americans and Hispanics, it wouldn't make a difference if the low-income population were green. Hustlers take advantage, because it's what they do. With our increasing Hispanic population, the Pimps and Hustlers made the patent hustler move: *"Se Hable Español."* You gotta give it to them, they're pretty slick and on "top of their game."[184]

Remember, last year Hustlers received about one billion ($1,000,000,000) in refund fees.[185] Which begs the question? If the Hustlers made all of this money from loan fees, how much money did they make from tax preparation?

As I said earlier, *Mo' Money, Mo' Money, Mo' Money!*[186] Tax is one of the biggest hustles I've ever seen and it's nonstop. Consider this, many of the RAL tactics reek of pimp-and drug dealers' transactions. For example:

---

184 "has everything under control"
185 *See* The Refund Tax Hustle, *Supra* cited at Footnote 178. (Citing H & R Block according to the National Consumer Law Center).
186 *See* The Wayans Brothers, *Supra* cited at Footnote 116.

Rule #1

"Make Sure That Your Product Is Known In The Streets"

In adhering to the #1 Hustler rule, these tax professionals advertise heavily to the masses in low-income neighborhoods, over air waves and billboards, offering their "generous" service of helping you get your money sooner. I've even seen Uncle Sam and the Statue of Liberty herself bidding you to come in and get that "Rapid Refund."[187]

And just when it couldn't get any worse, I saw an advertisement for free leather jackets if you prepare your taxes at their shop. *Unbelievable!*

I've heard rumor that if you bring your last paycheck in December, they can accelerate the process and you will have some money just in time for Christmas, Hanukkah, or Kwanzaa. *How generous, you really have these people's back.*[188]

Rule #2

NO REFUNDS

I'm not hating and I encourage everyone to get their "legitimate" hustle. One of the keys to hustling is like they say in a classic rock and roll song: "Take The Money and Run.[189]" Refunds are not in a Pimp's vocabulary.

What happens when the return is prepared incorrectly, because of a mathematical error or even a misunderstanding of the law? Many times the preparer is nowhere to be found; the taxpayer does not understand the tax complexities; and the IRS is sending certified letters. *"I knew that I shouldn't have trusted that gas station tax preparer."*

When you borrow the money, you run the risk of the IRS not accepting your return. If the IRS does not accept your return, then you'll have to

---

187   Liberty Tax Service employs the likeness of Uncle Sam and Lady Liberty. I've seen it myself.
188   Looking out for their best interest.
189   "Take The Money And Run." Single by The Steve Miller Band from the album *Fly Like An Eagle*. Released April 1976; Written and produced by Steve Miller. Label Capitol Records.

pay the Hustler (bank) back for the loan out of your grocery money. All of a sudden, *"No speak English."*

Help!!!!! All of this has got to be illegal! These Hustlers are charging outrageous rates; taking advantage of the poor; and not even attempting to reinvest in the communities they ransack.

Help is on the way. *Trumpet blowing.* Recently, several non-profit organizations petitioned Congress against the usurious RALs.[190] Their lobbying efforts resulted in several states passing laws regulating how tax preparers conduct business.[191]

Connecticut was the first state to address this issue.[192] No longer will the Pimps and Hustlers continue to rape and pillage their community. From here on out, the Connecticut Pimps and Hustler's fees are limited to sixty percent (60%).[193]

"What! Sixty percent (60%)! Thanks a lot! You're really looking out for my best interest. Instead of shanking[194] me with a six-inch blade, you gave me the four-inch. What a pal!"

Unfortunately, that's all the help you're gonna get and you better be rootin, tootin, glad you're getting it. You see, Connecticut is actually being pretty generous because Hustlers and Pimps could not run their game without the help of the Original Gangsta.

The Feds essentially allow Pimps and Hustlers to start their own Family for business purposes. The basis for the Family is the "Earned Income Tax." The Earned Income Tax Credit is one of the largest federal anti-poverty programs. Greater than fifty percent (50%) of all RAL customers were also recipients of the Earned Income Tax Credit.[195] *Things that make you go Hhmmm!*

---

190 *See* The Refund Tax Hustle, *Supra* cited at Footnote 178.
191 *Id.*
192 *Id.*
193 *Id.*
194 "stabbing"
195 *See* The Refund Tax Hustle, *Supra* cited at Footnote 178.

This is how it works. If you earned less than forty thousand dollars ($40,000.00), you may be eligible to claim a pre-determined credit on your tax return. *In English please?*

If you make less than forty thousand dollars ($40,000), instead of collecting taxes from you, the government is going to give you some cheese. And if you got crumb snatchers,[196] the government is going to make it worth your while exponentially. *You know, kinda like welfare.*

Depending on the circumstances, the more children you have, the larger the refund you receive. Naturally, this benefit leads to unscrupulous behavior such as selling children's social security numbers and falsifying tax filing statuses.

I have personally experienced it in my practice. All of a sudden, an individual's return goes from "Single" to "Head of Household," with five (5) dependents.

Yet, in spite of all of these generosities imposed by the Original Gangsta and the Feds, who is it that benefits the most . . . the Pimps and Hustlers. They continue doing business with the Godfather's blessings. Why? Because *"it's all about the cheddar, nobody do it better."*[197]

Thus, if you are eligible for an Earned Income Tax Credit and listen to Pimp Daddy, please understand he is actually padding his *own* pocket with the backing of the Original Gangsta. In the long run, if you waited for your refund, instead of electronically filing the RAL, you can purchase a 50" high definition television instead of a 42".

Interestingly, these Pimps and Hustlers are just like parasites. The worst part is, because of the yearly Original Gangsta filing ritual, the Pimps and Hustlers keep making, let's say it all together now: *"Mo' Money, Mo' Money, Mo' Money."*[198]

---

196   "Child" or "Children"
197   One who is extremely apt at raising financial capital. Taken from "Going Back To Cali" on the album "Life After Death" by Biggie Smalls. Written by C.Wallace, O. Harvey and Roger Troutman. Produced by "Easy Mo Bee. Released March 25, 1997. Label – Bad Boy.
198   *See* The Wayans Brothers, *Supra* cited at Footnote 116.

Choose a reputable tax preparer and don't, obtain a RAL. If you must have a refund, then deposit it directly into your bank account.

I've always heard that "game" recognizes "game." That is, it takes a "Pimp" to recognize a "Pimp." It takes a "Hustler" to recognize a "Hustler." In the first month of my business, I recognized what was going on and I was faced with two paths. Do I pimp our community and get pazzaid[199], or do I take the high road and educate our clients?

The decision making process didn't take very long; I took the high road. *Ding, Ding, Ding, one point for the attorneys of the world. At least one of those scum sucking, bottom feeders took the high road this one time, but let's keep an eye on him just in case. You know all of those attorneys look alike!*

The world is filled with Pimps and Hustlers. It's our job to expose them and enlighten those who wish to learn. As a good friend of mine says . . . "You can lead, where you can't go. You can't teach, what you don't know." Each One; Teach One.

---

199 "Paid."

THE BIG HUSTLE - HOW IT ALL BEGAN

BENJAMIN

CHAPTER SIX

From the beginning of civilized history, taxes have survived the test of time and I've heard during the Jurassic period, dinosaur meat was even taxed by the mega pound! The most amazing fact is taxes have existed in spite of the absence of:

- a money-based economy
- reasonably accurate accounts
- a common system of receipts, expenses and profits or
- even a civilized and orderly society with reliable records.[200]

Let's face it, taxes have been here since the beginning of time and they make the world go round. In the year 10, that's right year 10, Emperor Wang Mang of China instituted an unprecedented income tax, at the rate of ten percent (10%) of profits, for professionals and skilled labor.[201] Prior to this tax, all Chinese were subject to a head or property tax.[202]

You missed it! *"Prior to this."* This means taxes existed before the year 10. *Wow!* How many licks does it take to get to the core of the tax history tootsie pop? *"One, Two, Three. . . Three."*[203]

Fast forward. Many years later, (1798) William Pitt of Britain was feverously preparing for the Napoleonic wars and cash was running low.[204] Suddenly, he had an epiphany.

"I need some money to pay for weapons and war equipment to defeat those Napoleon Complex type people! I know what I'll do. I'll set up a two-stage plan: First, I'll create and implement a new system called an 'income tax.' Then, I'll use the media to sell the spin story and tell them

---

200   *See* Income Tax History; Wikipedia, The Free Encyclopedia (http://en.wikipedia.org/wicki/ Income_tax) (Retrieved 9.9.09.).

201   *Id.*

202   *Id.*

203   *See* Tootsie Roll Pops – Wikipedia, the free encyclopedia. http://en.wikipedia.org/wiki/ Tootsie_Pops. Tootsie Roll Pops are known for the catch phrase "How many licks does it take to get to the Tootsie Roll center of a Tootsie Pop?" This phrase became famous in 1970 after its animated commercial debuted. In the original television ad, a boy poses the question to a cow, a fox, a turtle and an owl. Each one of the first three animals tells the boy to ask someone else, explaining that they'd bite a Tootsie Pop every time they lick one. Eventually, he asks the owl, who starts licking it, but eventually bites into the lollipop, much to the chagrin of the boy.

204   *See* Income Tax History, *Supra* cited at Footnote 200.

the income tax is necessary to protect Bloody England and all of its rights and freedoms. Yeah, that's the ticket."

Little did William know his ingenuity would serve to establish a notorious precedent for funding many wars to come. History has repeatedly dictated that governments engage in war first and then figure out how to pay for them later. Let's take a look at how our modern income tax system began and how it spun out of control.

How It All Began

Christopher Columbus sailed the ocean blue and discovered America in 1492.[205] Well actually, Christopher Columbus did not discover America, John Cabot was the first to land in America.[206] To tell the truth, John Cabot was not the first to land because the first Europeans to reach the Americas were the Norse Vikings who established several colonies during the 11th century.[207]

Actually, if I recall correctly, what we know as America was originally inhabited by Native American Indians. Thus, asking the proverbial question how can you discover a land that is already inhabited? Proverbial answer; by force.

Anyway, Columbus, Cabot, Norse . . . *Boy, you know what your name is!* America was discovered and she implemented the golden rule . . . *"Divide and Conquer."*

By the late 16th century, the Portuguese and Spanish royal governments had established American settlements and American silver accounted for one-fifth (1/5th) of Spain's total budget.[208] The Spanish were pulling in the loot and the English wanted in on it. *"Hey, did you hear about the Spanish & Portuguese?" "Naw man, what's up?" "They're getting*

---

205 European Colonization of the Americas. http://en.wikipedia.org/wiki/European_colonization_of_the_Americas (7/23/2009).
206 *Id.*
207 *Id.*
208 *Id.* (Citing "Conquest In The Americas")

pazzaid on the silver tip." "Man, I gots to get in on that."

See, it's all motivated by "scrilla," "paper," and "cheese." As a Rap Artist once so prophetically proclaimed in a song . . . *"C.R.E.A.M.! Cash Rules Everything Around Me. CREAM! Get the money; dollar, dollar bill yall."*[209]

Driven by the "paper" the Spanish were receiving from the conquest of the Aztecs, Incas, and other large Native American populations, a few Englishmen decided to establish a permanent settlement in Jamestown, Virginia.[210] We've all been brainwashed to think that America was founded for "the sick, the poor and the huddled masses[211]" and it was. But, the real inspiration for the first English settlement was nothing more than the desire to get "pazzaid."[212] Basically, some English businessmen got together and invested time, energy and intellect with the hopes of receiving a substantial return on their investment.[213]

You see, these wealthy Englishmen understood the economic potential of this new land. Believe it or not, America as we know it was founded on the hope of finding gold or the possibility of finding a passage through the Americas to the Indies.[214]

From the beginning of Virginia's settlements, America's primary source of labor and most of its immigrants were indentured servants and debtor prisoners looking for new life in the overseas colonies.[215] Most of the servants and debtors were English farmers who had been pushed off their lands due to the expansion of raising livestock, the enclosure of

---

209   C.R.E.A.M. Wu-Tang Clan, Enter the Wu-Tang (36 Chambers) (Released November 9, 1993 on Loud Records) Distributed by RCA Records.

210   *See* European Colonization, *Supra* cited at Footnote 205.

211   Influence by the scripture on the Statute of Liberty. (Give me your tired, your poor, your huddled masses yearning to breathe free. Statue of Liberty, Wikipedia, the free encyclopedia (http://en.wikipedia.org/wiki/Statue_of_Liberty) (Retrieved 10.13.09).

212   "paid"

213   The Jamestown Settlement was sponsored by common stock companies such as the chartered Virginia Company and its off-shoot, the Somers Isle Company. *See* European Colonization, *Supra* cited at Footnote 205.

214   *Id.*

215   *Id.* Note: During the 17th century, indentured servants constituted three quarters of all European immigrants to the Chesapeake region.

land, and overcrowding in the countryside.[216] This unfortunate turn of events served as an impetus for hundreds of people (mostly single men) to leave the Motherland.[217] As it happens, the choice was actually pretty simple:

Sal: *"Johnny, what do we have behind Door #1?"*

Johnny: "For all of you wonderful prisoners we're offering you the adventure of a lifetime. Today and only until half pass the sand in the hour glass, Door #1 is offering the following:

- A fantastic cruise on a wooden boat across the Atlantic Ocean, meals and grog included.
- The opportunity to get in on the ground floor on a new and developing colony known as "America."
- Because we love and truly care about you, we will exonerate you of all crimes and you can start off with a clean slate after completing a mere five (5) to seven (7) years of indentured servitude;
- Last, but certainly not least, if you agree to these grand prizes, we will immediately release you from prison with a steak dinner and a new set of clothes."

Sal: *"And Johnny what do they get if they decide not to take Door #1?"*

Johnny: "Well Sal, they get to remain in prison or be forced from their homes; their bread and water rations reduced by half; and they will return to a dingy dungeon filled with rats, while accompanied by the grand opportunity of rotting in a cell for the rest of their lives."

Talk about easy choices!

---

216   *Id.*
217   *Id.*

In the 16th century about two hundred and forty thousand (240,000) Europeans entered American ports.[218] This influx of a new population produced goods and increased exporting and importing, while simultaneously maintaining established English customs.

Since the Brits were all about the paper,[219] they knew how to tax all of these activities and "get paid."[220] The Brits were making money hand over fist. *"Wait a minute; I don't understand how all of these activities are taxed? "Customs?"*

One of the most common British customs was, and still is, drinking tea in the morning, evening and night; with and without lemon, cream, or a shot of whiskey.

News Flash: America did not produce tea. Yet, the Americans had a tea fix[221] that needed scratching and the "monkey was on their back."[222] Like a heroin addiction, the question was, could these settlers kick the tea habit?

The Boston Tea Party

In 1773, the British Parliament passed the Tea Act imposing a tax on the tea shipped to the Americans.[223] Although the colonists enjoyed the tea, they objected strongly, because they believed it violated their right to be taxed only by their own elected representatives.[224]

Taxation without Representation? *Sounds familiar.* As a matter of fact,

---

218 *See* European Colonization, *Supra* cited at Footnote 205. (Citing: "The Columbian Mosaic in Colonial America" by James Axtell and "The Spanish Colonial System, 1550-1800. Population Development).

219 "money"

220 "receive remuneration"

221 A "fix" is a drug addiction mostly associated with heroin. *See* 1970 Black Exploitation Films. I recommend Shaft and Super Fly. For more modern movies see: "New Jack City" (Pookie *played by* Chris Rock) and "Sugar Hill" (1993) Directed by Leon Ichaso, Written by Barry Michael Cooper, Released February 25, 1994.

222 The "monkey on your back" is equivalent to having an addiction that you can't shake.

223 Boston Tea Party, From Wikipedia, The Free Encyclopedia (http://en.wikipedia.org/wiki/Boston_Tea_Party)(Retrieved 7.23.09) .

224 *Id.*

the last time I remember hearing that battle cry was by the residents of the District of Columbia.

Well, eventually the Americans had enough and the British were met with strong resistance. [225] In September and October of 1773, seven (7) ships carrying East India Company tea sailed for the colonies:

- Four (4) were bound for Boston
- One (1) for New York
- One (1) for Philadelphia and
- One (1) for Charleston. [226]

The ships were carrying approximately two thousand (2,000) chests containing nearly six hundred thousand (600,000) pounds of tea. [227] *Translation, a whole lot of "paper/scrilla."*[228] The British stood to make money not only from the selling of the tea, but also from the tax established by the Tea Act.

However, much to the British's surprise, they were met with protestors who successfully prevented the tea cargo from being unloaded. [229] Colony after colony, from Charleston all the way up to New York, the Americans refused to allow the British to deliver the tea. [230]

Obviously, tension was rising and the British could see their "paper" slipping away like a Georgia catfish greased in motor oil. So, they did what any legitimate hustler would do when his back is against the wall . . . they exercised force.

"Those damn Americans! I knew we shouldn't have let them out of debtor's prison. Truly, they have forgotten who they are dealing with. This tea cannot be returned. Somebody is going to buy this tea!"

---

225   *Id. See* Resisting The Tea Act.
226   *Id.*
227   *Id.* (quoting Labaree, Tea Party, 77, 335)
228   Money
229   *See* Boston Tea Party, *Supra* cited at Footnote 223.
230   *Id.*

Since Boston was the last port, it would prove to be the final battleground for the big showdown. The real deal is that the British were on the hook for the cargo of tea that they received from the British East India Company.[231] Either the colonists would pay for the tea (taxes included) or Britain would have to foot the bill.[232]

On the other side, the Americans grew weary of submitting to Britain's big thumb. The situation was escalated by the fact that the British Parliament was void of any direct American representation, yet the taxation continued without cease, compassion, or control.[233] So, the plot thickens.

Boston followed the lead of the other American colonies and refused to accept the tea.[234] Royal Governor Thomas Hutchinson refused to allow the tea to be returned to Britain.[235] However, the Governor underestimated the protestors and did not anticipate that the Americans would rather destroy the tea than concede to an authority void of any direct representation.[236]

One evening, after a town meeting held by Samuel Adams . . . *(Hey, ain't that the guy that makes the beer?)*, **Focus Daniel Son!**[237]

Sorry, Samuel Adams and some thirty (30) to one hundred and thirty (130) men, thinly disguised as Mohawk Indians, boarded three vessels and, over the course of three (3) hours, dumped all of the tea into the Boston Harbor near the foot of Hutchinson Street (today's Pearl Street).[238] The uncertainty of the number of men and exact location was indicative of how well the Americans were capable of "creeping."[239]

---

231 *Id.*
232 *Id.*
233 *Id.*
234 *Id.*
235 *Id.*
236 *Id.*
237 The Karate Kid, directed by John G. Avildsen, written by Robert Mark Kamen, produced by Jerry Weintraub, distributed by Columbia Pictures, release date June 22, 1984.
238 *See* Boston Tea Party, *Supra* cited at Footnote 223.
239 Moving in silence or the ability to see yet be unseen.

Parliament responded in 1774 with the Coercive Acts.[240] *"So, you wanna play rough, my friend. I'll show you rough. I'm gonna cut off your supply. Then, we'll see what kind of tough guy you are. I'll show you who's rough."*

The Coercive Acts closed Boston's commerce, until the Americans repaid the bill for the destroyed tea.[241] America responded with additional acts of protest.[242]

One of the American's most influential acts arising from the protest was the convening of the First Continental Congress.[243] And of course Congress' first agenda was petitioning the British monarch to repeal all acts and recognition of coordinated colonial resistance.[244] The crisis escalated and on March 5, 1770, a Black Man by the name of Crispus Attucks was shot by British soldiers. Therein began the American Revolution.[245]

In spite of the overwhelming odds, we spanked those Brits like they stole government stimulus money during a recession. But certainly, there was a financial price to pay? *War is expensive!*

Blood Is A Big Expense

In the "Godfather, Part I," a rivalry gang attempts an assassination on the Godfather. Although, he's still alive, he's hanging on by a mere thread. The assassination was ordered, because he refused to agree with the other families and expand the Mafia's business to drugs.[246]

---

240 *See* Boston Tea Party, *Supra* cited at Footnote 223.
241 *Id.*
242 *Id.*
243 *Id.*
244 *Id.*
245 Crispus Attucks, Wikipedia, the free encyclopedia; http/en.wikipedia.org/wiki/Crispus_ Attucks (Retrieved 10/2/09). "Court documents state that Attucks was the first one killed and that he took two bullets in the chest." As for the British Soldiers that committed the murder. John Adams argued self-defense and successfully defended the British soldiers against murder charges. Two of the soldiers were found guilty of manslaughter and because they were soldier of the King of England's army, they were given the choice of either death by hanging or branding of their thumbs. *Id.* Wow! Talk about easy choices.
246 *See* The Godfather, *Supra* cited at Footnote 153.

The Godfather enjoyed the police and politician's blind-eye consent to gambling and prostitution. He believed however, that "this narcotics business" was a beast of a different hide.

You've got to admire the Godfather. *"He may have indulged in creating gambling addictions and he was a corporate pimp of women, but he was not a drug dealer."*

Sollozo worked for the Tattagalia family and he had the job to either make the Godfather agree to the narcotics deal or rub him out. The Godfather made his choice not to sell drugs; so, Sollozo had his orders.

Well, to make a long story longer, Sollozo failed in his attempt to assassinate the Godfather, but he had one of the most classic lines of the movie. ***"Tom, I don't like violence. I'm a business man and blood is a big expense."***[247]

At the end of the American Revolution, our British Mother spent 8 million pounds and a national debt of 250 million pounds.[248] *Don't trip, it was no problem, "she a baddd girl."*[249] The Brits easily financed the debt at about 9.5 million pounds a year in interest.[250] *"I like the way they think!"*

The French spent about 1.3 billion livers (about 56 million pounds).[251] Their total national debt was 187 million pounds; however, it was not easily financed.[252] During the 1780s, over fifty percent of the French national revenue went to satisfy the outstanding debt service[253] and it was becoming a big issue:[254]
"Damn it. Every good thing comes from France. We can simply tax the people and generate more paper. Let them eat cake!" And that's

---

247   *Id.*
248   *See* American Revolutionary War, From Wikipedia, The Free Encyclopedia, (www.wikipedia. org/wiki/American_Revolutionary_War) (Retrieved 9.11.09)
249   "Has great power, wealth and influence."
250   *See* American Revolutionary War, *Supra* cited at Footnote 248.
251   *Id.*
252   *Id.*
253   *Id.*
254   *Id.*

exactly what the French did. They implemented taxes without public approval.[255] (Sound Familiar: "Taxation Without Representation"). Well, you know what happened next? The French Revolution![256]

The New Kids on the Block (Americans) played the game under the old adage, "you got to pay to play." The New Kids financed the war from a collective effort. Thirty-seven million dollars ($37,000,000) was spent at the national level and one hundred and fourteen million dollars ($114,000,000) was collectively spent by the States.[257]

This debt was utilized mostly to cover loans from France, the Netherlands, and some wealthy Americans.[258] And when that didn't work, the New Kids just produced and issued more "dummy paper." *Dummy paper?* "Fake", "counterfeit," "it ain't no good." But there's still a good side, *"there ain't be no taxes."*[259]

"The First American Hustle, Be It Known or Unknown"

These New Kids on the Block were unlike any other country in the world. The New Kid was a single reckoning force made up of individual parts, while contemporaneously possessing its respective governing authoritative functions. *"Yeah whatever, but the question remains, how we gonna get the money?"*

Alexander Hamilton took the lead. In an eight essay rebuttal to the Anti-Federalist, Hamilton insisted feverishly, that "A nation cannot long exist without revenues. Destitute of this essential support, it must resign its independence, and sink into the degraded condition of a province."[260] Hamilton assuaged public fears about the potential abuses of a direct tax by insisting that such a tax would rarely, if ever, be used.[261] "[I]t is

---

255   *Id.*
256   *Id.*
257   *Id.*
258   *Id.*
259   There weren't any taxes.
260   http://www.tax.org/Museum/1777-1815.htm, (1777 -1815 The Revolution War to the War of 1812; Tax History Museum) (Retrieved 8.15.2009).
261   *Id.*

evident," he noted, "from the state of the country, from the habits of the people, from the experience we have had . . . <u>that it is impractical to raise very considerable funds by direct taxation.</u>"[262]

Even though the revenue from tariff duties[263] constituted the bulk of federal revenue, Hamilton warned, despite this windfall, the national government <u>should not surrender the power of direct (or internal) taxation</u> to the States; it needed to retain a flexible set of options in the event of emergencies.[264]

You gotta love that Hamilton guy. He practices two of the fundamental rules of hustling: "Plan your next step before you implement your first" and "Always have an exit plan."

But surely Alexander didn't think that the country would be destitute forever. Otherwise, one should "relinquish their independence" and forgo the painstaking agony of building a new country.

Let's be real, this is the setting. You are responsible for formulating the financial and tax policies for a brand new country. Obviously, you have the best and the brightest think tanks your country has to offer. Amongst all of these geniuses, no one had the forethought to consider, "what if?"

- "What if" we can no longer depend on tariffs?
- "What if" we become the number one country in the world and need additional money to secure world peace?
- "What if" our population and revenue increased to a point that the destitute conditions that existed after the war are no longer and it is indeed practical to tax the public?
- "What if" we engage in a civil war?
- "What" if Britain gets "P-Od"[265] and decides to start another war?

---

262   *Id.* (Emphasis Added).
263   Tariffs are a duty levied on imported and/or exported goods. *See* www.Dictionary.com
264   *See* Boston Tea Party, *Supra* cited at Footnote 223.
265   Very Angry. Vengeful. Extremely Upset.

The War of 1812
(a.k.a. "The Second American Revolution")

In 1783, the Treaty of Paris was ratified and England recognized America as an independent country.[266] Naturally, tensions remained intense between the Mother Country and her offspring. However, the Brits "ain't no fool,"[267] so independence was accompanied by the right to engage in free trade.[268] *"I like those Brits, if you can't win, make sure you maintain a business relationship and make a quick buck.*

Since America was the New Kid on the Block, she wanted to expand westward and establish free trade with Europe.[269] *Here comes the drama!*

America wanted to trade with France; however, England was in a fierce struggle with France. Britain had fought a series of wars with France; thus, there was no love lost between the two.[270]

"Those low-down Americans; they're trying to play both hands towards the middle. They want to trade with us and with our enemy. We can't allow this madness to occur. Long Live England!"

As a result, Britain used its naval power to obstruct France's international trade; i.e. seizing American trade vessels.[271] Let's not forget that, less than a decade ago, Britain was fighting the American Revolutionary War. Her humiliating loss to this "unknown" toiled heavily on morale[272] and everybody proclaimed England a fake.[273] England was losing Her recognition as the supreme world power. There

---

266 Causes of the War of 1812 The Reasons Behind the Second American Revolution © **Brian Tubbs Feb 1, 2008** (Sources: 1812: The War That Forged a Nation by Walter Borneman, How America Got it Right by Bevin Alexander Online Resource: "James Madison's War Message" History Channel DVD: First Invasion - The War of 1812

267 "Are very smart"

268 *See* Causes of the War of 1812, S*upra* cited at Footnote 266.

269 *Id.*

270 *Id.*

271 *Id.*

272 *Id.*

273 England had lost its status as supreme ruler of the known worlds.

was a kink in the amour and now the once mighty British Royal Navy was suffering the ill affects of deserting seamen. [274]

To make matters worst, the deserters were fleeing to American ships. [275] *"You gonna leave and go fight for our enemy, Oh, Hell No."* The Brits began seizing American trade vessels and forcing American seamen to join your Majesty's Royal Navy. [276]

In response, President James Madison petitioned Congress to declare war on the British Empire. [277] Mr. Madison's speech focused heavily on "Britain's complete disregard of US sovereignty on the high seas." *In other words, we kicked England's butt and they "not respecting nor recognizing."* [278] Congress agreed and the Americans declared war against her Mother (Britain) again. [279]

You would think that a parent knows when it's time to release a child into the world. No, not England. The War of 1812 lasted approximately three years. [280] Though it ended in more or less a stalemate, the United States established itself as a worthy member of the family of nations, captured a newfound nationalism, and would never again face such an overt threat to its sovereignty. [281]

----*"Hey Pal, sorry to interrupt the story. By the way, thanks a lot for the great history lesson, but I thought that we were talking about taxes."* You're right my friend; let's take a look at the backdrop.

---

274   *See* Causes of the War of 1812, *Supra* cited at Footnote 266.

275   *Id.*

276   *Id.* Moreover, the British Empire hoped to restrain US expansion into the western frontier. It was simply not in the best interests of Britain's remaining North American colony, Canada, for the United States to expand unimpeded to the Pacific Ocean. Accordingly, Britain and Canada supported Indian tribal nations in their resistance to US expansionism. This included an alliance with the charismatic Indian leader Tecumseh.

277   *Id.*

278   Britain is not acknowledging America's sovereignty.

279   *Id.*

280   *Id.*

281   *Id.*

The Big Hustle
1ˢᵗ Attempt

After the war of 1812, the New Kids on the Block had accumulated a staggering debt of $100 million smakaroos and they didn't even have France or the Netherlands to back them up.[282] Initially, America financed the war by doubling the rates of its major source of revenue, customs duties on imports.[283] This strategy was overall ineffective, because it obstructed trade and was eventually a revenue generating failure compared to previous lower rates.[284]

At the height of the war, excise taxes were imposed on goods and commodities.[285] For the first time, housing, slaves, and land were taxed.[286] By the end of the war, these taxes were repealed and instead a high tariff was passed to retire the accumulated war debt.[287] *So far, so good. No Income Tax!*

The Bigger Hustle
Attempt #2

After the War of 1812, the New Kids on the Block would celebrate their independence every July 4ᵗʰ. Well, everything was going pretty good until word got around about some rebellious Southerners singing about "land of cotton" and how they "wish[ed] they were in Dixie. Hooray, Hooray."[288] This singing led to the cannon firing in Sumter, South Carolina thereby leading to the South's succession from the Union.[289] Herein lies the rub: The Civil War was expensive, costing on average,

282   The Origin of the Income Tax, Ludwing von Mises Institute; Mises Daily Written By Adam Young; Posted 09.07.04; 12:00:00 a.m. www.mises.org/story/1597 (Retrieved 9.6.09).

283   *Id.*

284   *Id.*

285   *Id.*

286   Is this the first time?

287   *See* The Origin of the Income Tax, *Supra* cited at Footnote 282.

288   "Dixie" also known as "I Wish I Was In Dixie." According to tradition, Ohio born minstrel show composer Daniel Decatur Emmett wrote "Dixie" around 1859, quoting Asimov, Chronology of The World. *See* http://en.wikipedia.org/wiki/Dixie (Song) (Retrieved May 2, 2010).

289   Sumter, South Carolina, Wikipedia, the free encyclopedia (http://en.wikipedia.org/wiki/Sumter,_SC) (Retrieved 10.12.09)

one million, seven hundred and fifty thousand dollars ($1,750,000) per day.[290] *Guess what happened?* That's right, funds started to get low.[291]

To satisfy expenditures, the Republican Congress borrowed heavily, doubled tariff rates, sold off public lands, imposed a maze of licensing fees, increased old excise tax rates and created new excise taxes.[292] *"Jesus, why don't you just take my first born and get it over with already?"*

Believe it or not, none of this was enough. Financing the Civil War was costing a little more than anticipated. *Sound familiar?*

In order to fund the Civil War and ensure that those Southern Rebels didn't succeed, Congress created the first American income tax in 1861.[293] Congress initially placed a flat three-percent (3%) tax on all incomes over eight hundred dollars ($800).[294] *Three percent (3%)! That ain't too bad. But, boy does it get even more gooder.*[295]

Later, Congress modified the law, included a graduated tax and in 1872, the income tax law expired. Again, America was without an income tax.[296] *"What a wonderful country! This America place rocks. The North rules and the South drools."*

Well, the North did win, but the concept of the income tax just wouldn't go away. In 1894, as part of a high tariff bill, Congress enacted a two percent (2%) tax on incomes over four thousand dollars ($4,000).[297] Interestingly enough, several salaries were exempted, including: State and Local Officials, Federal Judges and the President.[298] However, the

---

290 *Id.*

291 *Id.*

292 *Id.*

293 Amendments To The US Constitution, <u>ClassBrain.com</u>, Defining Documents of the United States, (http:www.classbrain.com/artteenst/publish/16th_amendment.shtml) (Retrieved 5.21.09).

294 *See* The Origin Of The Income Tax, *Supra* cited at Footnote 282.

295 "better"

296 *See* Amendments To the US Constitution, *Supra* cited at Footnote 293.

297 *Id.*

298 *Id.*

Big Kahuna (Supreme Court) immediately struck it down by a five to four decision.[299]

Apparently, the Supreme Court upheld the validity of income taxes for the war but not for commerce. Remember, initially the Big Kahuna upheld the constitutionality of the Civil War Tax, but now it was a no go.[300]

The Biggest Hustle
Attempt #3
(Third Time Is A Charm)

In 1909, Congress tried again.[301] There was a tariff bill on the floor and the "progressives" attempted to piggy back the bill and attach a provision for an income tax.[302]

The "conservatives," hoping to kill the idea for good, proposed a constitutional amendment enacting the tax.[303] Although the idea was simple, they out thunk[304] themselves.

A Constitutional Amendment requires ratification by three fourths (3/4) of the States and they were convinced that this would never happen. To the conservatives' surprise, the amendment was ratified.[305]
One by one, each State ratified the amendment[306] like a plethora of dominoes falling in succession one after another. On February 25, 1913, with the certification of Secretary of State, Philander C. Knox, the Sixteenth (16th) Amendment took effect.[307]

But all was not lost. In April of the same year, Congress passed an

---

299　*Id.*
300　*Id.*
301　*Id.*
302　*Id.*
303　*Id.*
304　"out thought"
305　*See* The Origin Of The Income Tax, *Supra* cited at Footnote 282.
306　*Id.*
307　*Id.*

income tax on all incomes greater than three thousand dollars ($3,000.
00). In addition, surcharges between two percent (2%) to five percent
(5%) were applied on incomes from twenty thousand dollars ($20,000)
to half a million dollars ($500,000.)[308]

With each passing year, the income slowly increased without the general
population ever truly realizing what was happening. A percentage here
and a pinch there and after a while, no one noticed the increase.

In typical gangster fashion, Congress made several strong arm moves
early in the game to increase compliance:

- In 1864, Americans had to swear for the first time to the veracity
  of their tax returns. *(I never knew we had to swear to the
  veracity? Check the small print. As they always say, the large
  print giveth and the small print taketh away).*
- Government assessors could challenge a return.
- The penalty for not filing a tax return doubled to ten percent
  (10%).
- The IRS could make tax returns available to the press.[309] *"Don't
  mess with us, we'll put your business in the streets. We'll make
  it so that you'll never work in this town again." That's just
  low down!* This practice was outlawed in 1870. Thank God for
  separation of powers.

At first (1914), the revenue raised by the new income tax was
disappointing; only twenty-eight million dollars ($28,000,000) was
generated.[310] The next year, the income tax generated forty-one million
dollars in revenue ($41,000,000), when the top rate was seven percent
(7%). In 1916, the income tax was raised to fifteen percent (15%)
and generated nearly seventy-eight million dollars ($78,000,000).[311]
Eventually, more than one billion ($1,000,000,000) of income tax was
raised during World War I. In 1917, the income tax rates escalated to

---

308 *Id.*
309 *Id.*
310 *Id.*
311 *Id.*

sixty-seven percent (67%) and in 1918, it increased to seventy-seven percent (77%). [312] *Wow!*

After the "War to End Wars," the top rate fell to seventy-three percent (73%). [313] In the 1920's, the income tax rates fell as low as twenty-four percent (24%), but never again would we reach an all time low of the pre-war seven percent (7%). [314] *What wouldn't we do for a seven percent (7%) rate today?*

Mr. Hoover and the Republicans raised the rate to twenty-five percent (25%) in 1930, then to sixty-three percent (63%) in 1932. [315] Under the corporate statism of the New Deal, rates leaped to seventy-nine percent (79%) in 1936. In 1944-45, the income tax rate reached an all time high of ninety-four percent (94%). [316] *Maybe we shouldn't complain?*

In 1939, the income tax raised one billion dollars ($1,000,000,000). [317] Sixteen (16) years later it would raise nineteen billion dollars ($19,000,000,000.) [318] *Again, as my Sister would say, "what had happen?"*

Answer: The government found a fertile harvest with the middle and working class taxpayers. [319] As Chief Justice John Marshall remarked, truly "the power to tax involves the power to destroy." [320] *Ain't that the truth, Ruth!*

The income tax lived up to its nature during World War II, devouring American wealth and liberties like a swarm of locusts. [321]

---

312 *Id.*
313 *Id.*
314 *Id.*
315 *Id.*
316 *Id.*
317 *Id.*
318 *Id.*
319 *Id.*
320 *Id.*
321 *Id.*

The Move of All Moves (Gangsta!)

In 1943, the government began withholding taxes on the advice of Milton Friedman.[322] *"Excellent Question! What is "withholding?"*

Withholding is when the government takes your money, for spending or investing purposes, "before," I repeat "before" your tax is calculated or even paid. Then, they make you submit a form to receive any extra money that is above your tax.

Let's not forget the most important part . . . an "interest free" loan to the government. Oh yeah, one more thing, if the IRS does not agree with the amount you submitted, then it has the right to audit you with the full backing of the federal government. And trust me, the federal government has "long paper."[323] As my Father would say, *"You can fight all day when you have long paper."*

The great income tax critic Frank Chodorov wrote "whichever way you turn this amendment you come up with the fact that it gives the government a prior lien on all the property produced by its subjects."[324] That is, before you make the money, the IRS already has the right to assess, tax, and collect/seize it if necessary.

Wow, what a novel concept. Our Congressmen created a new vehicle to fund wars. Actually, the concept is not so novel. Remember our friend William Pitt.

But you gotta give it to the New Kids on the Block. They figured out a way get the money now instead of later. *Genius, sheer Genius!*

After the war ended, this method of stealth taxation and tax increases obviously continued. In 1964 the top rates were lowed to seventy-seven percent (77%).[325] In 1982, the top rate was lowered to fifty percent (50%)

---

322 *Id.*
323 A lot of cheese, dough, money, scrilla.
324 *See* The Origin Of The Income Tax, *Supra* cited at Footnote 282.
325 *Id.*

and by the late 1980's the rate was lowered to twenty-eight percent (28%).[326]

Rates were raised again to thirty-one percent (31%) under President George W. Bush. In 1993, the rates were raised to thirty-nine percent (39%) under President William J. Clinton.[327] Currently, the top marginal tax rate is thirty-five percent (35%).

In 1940, approximately fifteen million (15,000,000) tax returns were filed.[328] Just ten years later, the tax returns filed increased to fifty-three million (53,000,000).[329] Today, the IRS receives over one hundred and thirty-five million, three hundred and sixty-two thousand, six hundred and seventy eight (135,362,678) returns annually.[330] Yet, let us not forget that this number represents *personal income taxes exclusively*. It does not include partnership, corporations, S-corporations, etc.

In the 2008 tax year, the Internal Revenue Service collected 2.7 trillion dollars.[331] No wonder our government can give away millions with ease. Millions ain't jack when you got Trillions with a Capital "T."

History Note: April 15th has not always been the filing deadline. March 1st was the original date specified by Congress in 1913 after the passage of the Sixteenth (16th) Amendment.[332] In 1918, Congress pushed the date forward to March 15th.[333] When the 1954 tax overhaul occurred, the filing date was moved to April 15th.[334]

However, we can't say that we were not warned. Every generation has a Nostradomus. Richard E. Byrd warned us about this gangster regime we endure. During the time, Mr. Byrd was the Speaker of the

---

326 *Id.*
327 *Id.*
328 *Id.*
329 *Id.*
330 http://wiki.answers.com/Q/How_many-taxpayers_are_in_the_us. (Retrieved May 7, 2010).
331 Tax Policy Center (http://www.taxpolicycenter.org/taxfacts/ContentGIF/state_irs.gif
332 History Of The US Income Tax, the Library of congress, Business Reference Services. (www.loc.gov/rr/business/hottopic/irs_history.html) (Retrieved 7.3.2009)
333 *Id.*
334 *Id.*

Virginia House of Delegates, and he succinctly predicted that a "hand from Washington will be stretched out and placed upon every man's business . . . Heavy fines imposed by distant and unfamiliar tribunals will constantly menace the taxpayer. An army of Federal officials, spies and detectives will descend upon the state . . ."[335] *Pandora has opened the proverbial box.*

I learned an invaluable hustler lesson from a movie called "The Sting,"[336] starring Robert Redford and Paul Newman. Never let the mark realize that they've been hustled, bamboozled or hoodwinked. It's all part of an elaborate scheme.

Today, the Big Hustle continues in full effect. Years turn into decades; decades turn into a generation; and a generation turns into generations. Alas, Nirvana. You have generations who continue to pay taxes and receive a refund, thinking they've actually received something; when in fact they've done nothing more than give the government an interest free loan. (*See* "The Proverbial Question").

The Big Hustle continues like a well-oiled machine, stopping for nothing or no one. Is our tax system fair? *Probably not.*

Is it perfect? *"Hell No."* Is it effective? *You know it is.* Can we improve it? *Definitely!* How? *I have no idea!*

I do know that the first step is communication. Since everyone is affected by taxes, then the discussion should include everyone. Maybe if we all understood the system and knew where the money was allocated, perhaps we would have a different attitude. Nonetheless, each one of us has a civic duty and we owe it to ourselves and our future generations to investigate, comprehend and improve our federal government and society in general.

---

335 *See* The Origin Of The Income Tax, *Supra* cited at Footnote 282.

336 The Sting. *See* Wikipedia, the free encyclopedia. Directed by George Roy Hill; Produced by: Tony Bill, Michael Phillips, Julia Phillips; Written by: David S. Ward; Starring Paul Newman, Robert Redford, Robert Shaw, Charles Durning; Music by: Marvin Hamlisch; Release Date December 25, 1973; Film Poster by Richard Amsel. (http://en.wikipedia.org/wiki/The_Sting)(Retrieved 8.20.10).

As long as there is life, critics will exist. There are some who say "taxes are unconstitutional and we shouldn't have to pay anything." There are others who think that the "Fair Tax"[337] is the right way. There are even some who are willing to lie, cheat and steal to avoid paying taxes. Excluding the lying, cheating and stealing, the answer, like most good compromises, is somewhere in the middle.

I also know we can never[338] stop trying to build a better mouse trap. The day we become compliant is the day we're truly lost. Yet, the biggest challenge is the great majority of us don't understand the system; yet, we subconsciously comply like mindless zombies in a Michael Jackson "Thriller" video.[339]

Maybe a component of the answer is to hold the government and ourselves accountable. What would happen if the IRS opened its books? Its intimidation strangle hold would dissipate like sand in an hour glass. With transparency comes knowledge, and with knowledge comes power. Knowledge of the Original Gangsta would expose inefficiencies like: mathematical errors; insufficient and inadequate staff; and flawed policies. America as we know it would change forever. If we enter the transaction with our eyes opened, perhaps we won't fall for the Big Hustle again. *And to put it simply, that's what had happen[340] and how it all began!*

---

337   The **FairTax** is a proposed change to the federal government tax laws of the United States intended to replace all federal income taxes[1] with a single broad national consumption tax on retail sales. *See* Wikipedia, the free encyclopedia (http://en.wikipedia.org/wiki/FairTax)(Retrived 10.20.10).

338   Never is word that is never used except in certain foundational principles like "Never Quit."

339   Michael Jackson's Thriller. From Wikipedia, the free encyclopedia. Directed by John Landis; Produced by George Folsey Jr.; Written by: John Landis & Michael Jackson; Starring Michael Jackson, Ola Ray, and Vincent Price; Release Date December 2 1983; Budget US $500,000; Sales 9 million units. (http://en.wikipedia.org/wiki/Michael_Jackson%27s_Thriller) (Retrieved 8.20.10). Note: Have you ever compared "Thriller" to "Dawn of the Dead." The similarities are uncanny.

340   "what happened"

GET YOUR
MIND RIGHT!

ZEBULUN

CHAPTER SEVEN

I dare say that the majority of US Taxpayers do not have their minds right. They mindlessly participate in an annual ritual designed to raise revenue to ensure that we live in a "civilized society."[341]

This ambivalence is due to the complexity of the tax law, compounded by the Original Gangsta's intimidating nature. *"Okay let me get this straight, I have to file last year's taxes the next year before April 15th, unless I file an extension; however, the interest will continue to accrue even though the extension has been granted." Uggghh. It seems wrong, wrong, wrong and they don't love Jesus.*

Unfortunately, until another Boston Tea Party and more, we're stuck with what we got. In the interim, since our system won't change, "we must change." In other words, we will obtain our success by mindfully and spiritually working from inside the system.

Working from the inside the system is not reflective of a submissive attitude. We're attacking it like a pack of African wild dogs that haven't eaten in two weeks during the dry season on the Serengeti.

Tax is a proactive contact sport . . . kind of like playing a defensive back in the NFL. That is, you have to bring the heat; you can't wait for the heat to come to you. When the wide receiver catches the ball, the defensive back's job is to hit the receiver so hard as to make him drop the ball or think about dropping the ball the next time it's thrown in his direction.

For those of you who are not football fans, "bringing the heat" is synonymous to full contact "ultimate fighting." You can use your knees and elbows as weapons; the eyes can be gouged; and everything else is open game. *"Lions, and Tigers and Bears. Oh My!"*[342]

How can we do this when so few of us truly understand how taxes work?

---

341 On the top of the former IRS headquarters at 1111 Constitution Avenue, NW Washington, DC are inscribed the following words by Oliver Wendell Holmes: "Taxes Are What We Pay For A Civilized Society."

342 Wizard of Oz, *Supra* at "But Paying Taxes Is Unconstitutional" cited at Footnote 100.

This is my calling and if you continue to read, I can guarantee you will "Get Your Mind Right" despite all of the "false evidence appearing real" (FEAR).[343]

How do we put ourselves in the best possible tax situation, while simultaneously satisfying our biblical obligations to "Render Unto Caesar ... But Nothing More?" Unfortunately, this process requires intense concentration, constant reiteration, unending amounts of study, and physical toil beyond comprehension.

It mandates memorizing countless tax laws; analyzing them with the facts; and making unimaginable efforts to distinguish or compare the given facts to the rule of tax law promulgated by these United States. You must have the courage of a lion and the stealth of a crocodile.

---

343   Mrs. Jaye Tillman (Awesome Lady) Atlanta, GA

NOT!

Well, maybe you do need the heart of a lion and the stealth of a crocodile. However, the process of "Getting Your Mind Right" is as simple as 2 + 2 = 4; it's as fluid as running water over a gentle waterfall; and as easy as just letting go. So, if you're expecting a legal/mathematical thesis, based on the great minds of our time and how such tax laws were so eloquently pontificated, it just "ain't[344]" there. The answer is just a matter of getting connected. If you get connected with God, I guarantee[345] that you will "Get Your Mind Right."

OMG[346], there he goes again talking about that God stuff. How can God possibly help me with taxes? I wish that he would just stick to the tax stuff.

As my young friends say, *"Don't get it twisted[347]."* God **can** help you with your taxes! God is Omnipotent, Omnipresent, and Omniscient. Believe it or not, these big three "Os" encompass the entire subject of tax.

As the old timers say: "He's your doctor in a hospital and He's your lawyer in the courtroom." Well, this time the lawyer just happens to practice tax. If you "get connected" with God, then He can be your tax lawyer. If you believe, then He will bring you every resource you need.

If you "get connected" with God, then He can be your tax lawyer. If you believe, then He will bring you every resource you need.

For some, "getting connected" may be the very words that you're reading; for others, it may be a seminar that makes the light bulb burst; and for others, it may be the unfortunate day that you receive a certified letter from the Internal Revenue Service. To paraphrase a saying I once heard,

---

344   "isn't"
345   Candidly, I had trouble making a guarantee because intrinsically, I'm still a great white shark like the other tax attorneys. But, I can guarantee that if you connect with God, then you will "Get Your Mind Right."
346   "Oh My God"
347   "don't be confused."

"not getting connected hasn't helped the situation[348], so you might as well try it."

The Bible *sazzzzz,*[349] "now faith is the substance of things hoped for; the evidence of things unseen."[350] Your first step to resolving all of your tax issues is having faith that God will bring you the knowledge, understanding, and application for your unique tax situation.

More importantly, do you have enough faith to believe that God will improve your tax positioning not only for today or tomorrow, but for five years from now? What about until death do us part? What about generationally? Certainly, if there are generational curses, there can also be generational blessings.

But let's not forget that faith alone is not enough. Again, the Bible *sazzzzz,*[351] "faith without works is dead."[352] Works is the second step in getting connected. *Wait a minute; I thought you said that we didn't have to do all of that intellectual mumbo jumbo mental gymnastics?*

No, my friend, mental gymnastics are not necessary; however, we gotta do some kind of work, but I promise it ain't hard. The first step of the work process is, "Pay Attention to the Man Behind the Curtain." Everyday, the Wizard is peeking through the curtain to see if you are shaking in your boots and frightened by the green floating head.

He's hoping that you don't realize that it's just an illusion. The illusion is, as US citizens, we are not required to pay more taxes than legally obligated. "Works" requires the adaptability and flexibility of a

---

348 Paraphrasing a saying by "A Pimp Named Slickback" from the "Boondocks" TV Series. Producers: Brian Ash & Seung Eun Kim. Production Company: Sony Pictures Television. Original Run November 6, 2005 – present). *See* The Boondocks (TV Series) –Wikipedia, the free encyclopedia, (http://en.wikipedia.org/wiki/The_Boondocks_(TV series). (Retrieved 3.15.2012). A Pimp Named Slickback (voiced by Katt Williams) is a pimp who becomes easily irritated when called "Slickback" for short. Although he appeared in several episodes, the paraphrased saying is from a Season 2 episode "Tom, Sarah & Usher." *See* also List of the Boondocks characters –Wikipedia, the free encyclopedia (http://en.wikipedia.org/wiki/A_Pimp_Named_Slickback) (Retrieved 3.15.2012).

349 "says"

350 Hebrews 11:1 (New Revised Standard)

351 "says"

352 James 2:26 KJV

chameleon. Because society is constantly changing, the tax laws are also in a constant state of flux. Works requires always knowing what's going on and exploiting the appropriate deficiencies.

We must adapt like *cocka* roaches that have survived the test of time. We must expand our minds; read between the lines; find the holes; and manipulate them accordingly.

The million dollar question is, "**How much are we suppose to render?**" In this question lies the wiggle room. You say "potato," I say "potatoe.[353]" You say "income," I say "loan." You say "employee," I say "independent contractor."

The only way that we can truly play the game is to realize that taxes are nothing more than a game. If however you don't know that you're in a game, how can you possibly win? "You can't." Most of us are at the whims of the Original Gangsta and paying far more tax than we should.

Since neither man, woman, or child is perfect, then it is impossible for our laws to be anything but imperfect. My job is to encourage clients to exploit any such imperfections and legally comply.

Our next step comes to us from Sun-Tzu's "The Art of War:"

> Prior information will enable wise rulers and worthy generals to move and successfully conquer the multitudes. This information cannot be obtained or deducted from divination,[354] analogy; or measurement. It can only be obtained from men who know the enemy's disposition.[355]

---

353   Vice President Dan Quayle corrected a child's spelling of "potato" by spelling it "potatoe" (*See* http://www.urbandictionary.com/define.php?term=potatoe).

354   Sun-Tzu original text uses the word "spirits." Mei Yaochen's further expounds to discuss those spirits that are sought through divination. Infra.

355   The Art of War (The essential translation of the classic book of life), Espionage PP 90 & 316. Written by Sun-Tzu. Edited, Translated by John Minford. Published by Penguin Books. Copyright 2002.

Sun-Tzu instructs that prior information is clearly critical to successful warfare. This information has the power to snatch victory out the jaws of defeat. It can only be obtained; however, from men (and women) who "know the enemy's disposition."[356]

Know Your Enemy

Well, this one is easy. As you know, I served with the Original Gangsta as one of their many Consigliores; hence, I know its ways. Its thoughts are my thoughts and its ways are my ways.[357] Since I was the enemy, I know the enemy.

We all know that the IRS is the "Original Gangsta." The real question is, how does the Original Gangsta operate? The Original Gangsta is built on a rack of rules, regulations, court cases, and compliance policies. Actually, other than the Catholic Church, there probably has not been a greater display of supreme organization and command.

At the IRS, the Internal Revenue Code is the Bible and supreme authority. The Internal Revenue Code is divided into sections, with laser point precision. Those sections are divided into sections, and so on and so on.

A massive group of tax experts work like a well-oiled machine with respect to each section of the Internal Revenue Code. This well-oiled machine has one mission . . . "gettin that paper over and over again;" that is, collecting the money.

Most of us think the auditors and examiners are the bad people. Actually, auditors and examiners are only the muscle of the Service. They go out, get the money, and bring it back to the house.

---

356 *Id.*

357 Paraphrase of Isaiah 55:8-9. ("for my thoughts are not your thoughts, neither are your ways my ways, saith the LORD. For as the heavens are higher than the earth, so are my ways higher than your ways, and my thoughts than your thoughts.

The baddest people in the Service are the Gestapo. *Are they badder than "Shaft?" You damn right!*[358] Note: Even though they may be "badder" than Shaft, they are not nearly as cool.[359]

The Gestapo is made up of "G" Men/Women (collectively referred to as "G Men") dedicated to the efficiency of specific tax programs. The G Men are the captains of the family and they insure that the tax collection machine operates at full throttle. The Gestapo executes the Original Gangsta's policies through enforcement of the machine and society[360] itself.

"Interesting question, I'm glad you asked." If the Gestapo G-Men are the captains, "Who is the Godfather?" Though your question is intriguing, I think what you really meant to ask is *"Who are the Godfathers?"* The Godfathers are: the President ("El Presidente"); Congress ("The Don") and the Supreme Court ("The Big Kahuna"). Although each Godfather has its separate family, they all work inextricably, hand in hand, to execute, promulgate, and interpret our tax laws.

The Don drafts the statutes that eventually make their way to the Internal Revenue Code. Most of the time everything works out; however, sometimes there's a taxpayer who proclaims, *"Taxes are unconstitutional and damn it, I'm not going to take it anymore!"*

After satisfying the lower courts' jurisdictions, the case eventually makes it way to the "The Big Kahuna." This is where the rubber meets the road. Ultimately, the Big Kahuna determines whether the statute will live or die. The Big Kahuna interprets the statutes and dictates how the masses will conform to society's rules. Paying taxes is one of those rules.

Once the Big Kahuna renders its decision, El Presidente' makes sure that our tax laws are executed vis-a-vie, the Original Gangsta. The

---

358   Shaft is an American Blaxploitation film directed by Gordon Parks; produced by Joel Freeman; written by Ernest Tidyman (novel & screenplay) & John D.F. Black; released by Metro-Goldwyn-Mayer on July 2, 1971 (USA). Starring Richard Roundtree as "Shaft." Soundtrack by Isaac Hayes. Isaac Hayes won an American Academy Award for the Best Original Song with the song "Theme From Shaft." You dog gone skippy! That's right, Shaft was all of that and a bag of hot funyuns.
359   Intentionally left blank!
360   Society's implications are discussed in "A Conversation With Mrs. Service."

Original Gangsta is actually the strong arm of the Godfathers. *Why?* El Presidente's family is responsible for collecting the paper.[361]

Eventually, someone challenges El Presidente's family; they go to see the Big Kahuna, and the process starts all over again. The only way to change the tax laws is for The Don to promulgate a new law. And then . . . *here we go again.*

I am thankful for the inside knowledge that God and the Original Gangsta blessed me with, but it was a great sigh of relief when I left. The Original Gangsta is actually harder on its own people than the general public. If an IRS employee is late filing his/her return, including extensions, it is immediate grounds for dismissal.[362]

Actually, when you think about this, it makes sense. If word got out that the Original Gangsta couldn't make its own people comply, then it would lose respect and, as we know, respect is the first and only thing every true gangsta has. Thereby bringing us to the inevitable conclusion, if the Original Gangsta don't[363] give a damn about its own people, you know that it don't[364]give a damn about Joe and Jane Taxpayer. **Well, what the Hell is[365] we suppose to do?**

Don't despair. We must first, look out for ourselves and adhere to the first law of nature: "self-preservation." We must get our minds right and think creatively.

We definitely know that tax season doesn't begin on the April 15th filing deadline and that it definitely does not end on October 15th. It actually begins the prior year. When you get your mind right, you've planned your tax liability years in advance.

We must go beyond the smoke and mirrors, beyond the horse and pony

---

361 "money"
362 *See* Public Law 105-206 – Internal Revenue Service, restructuring and Reform Act of 1998. §1203
363 "doesn't"
364 *Id.*
365 "are"

show, and see what's really going on. To my amazement, after the smoke cleared, the Original Gangsta operates much like a child's game. You know the one where there are two identical pictures of: Old Farmer Joe, Miss Maid, James the Storekeeper, etc.; all of the cards are placed face down; and you turn one over and then another, in an attempt to match. That's right, the Original Gangsta is playing the "Matching Game" with our valuable tax dollars.

THE MATCHING GAME
(a.k.a. Old Farmer Joe)

Don Corleone is in retirement and his son Michael is serving as the Godfather.[366] Don Barzini and other rival families are feverishly licking their chops for an opportunity to take over the Corleone Family.[367] Although Barzini had plans to assassinate Michael, Don Corleone saw the plot a mile away.[368] While reminiscing with great sincerity and introspection, Don Corleone tells Michael, *"Now listen, whoever comes to you with this Barzini meeting, he's the traitor. Don't forget that!"*[369]

Now I tell you, if nothing else, *don't forget this!* The Original Gangsta's total foundation is built on the Matching Game. *"Naa, get outta here. You trying to tell me that the Original Gangsta operates on that old nursery game where you turn cards over to try and match them?"* Yes, that's right my good friend, the crux of the Internal Revenue Service is built on the *Old Farmer Joe, Old Maid,* "Matching Game."

At the end of the year, your employer provides you with a W-2 and, for educational purposes, let's name this W-2, *"Old Farmer Joe."* *Old Farmer Joe* tells us the following information:

- Gross Income (*Money, Cheddar, Paper, Dough accumulated during the year*)
- Federal Income Taxes Withheld (*The Original Gangsta's cut*)

---

366   *See* The Godfather, *Supra* cited at Footnote 153.
367   *Id.*
368   *Id.*
369   *Id.*

- FICA (Social Security) and Medicare (*Please! I've been working since I was fourteen (14) and I gave up any hopes of receiving social security in the 80's.*")
- State Taxes (*Junior Mafia*)

Ironically, your employer also provides the Original Gangsta with an identical copy of "*Old Farmer Joe.*" And, what do you know, "*Old Farmer Joe*" was also issued to your State Department of Revenue and your employer kept a copy.

When you file your income tax return and attach "*Old Farmer Joe,*" the Original Gangsta makes sure that your "*Old Farmer Joe*" matches their "*Old Farmer Joe.*" If everything matches . . . "que bueno[370]." However, if it doesn't match, then there's hell to pay!

But remember, if *Old Farmer Joe* doesn't match, then you're already at a great disadvantage. *Huh?* Under the best case scenario, the Original Gangsta is not going to review your return for at least a year. During this time, interest and penalties are ticking with the passing of each day.

Interest and Penalties! But it was a mistake and taxes are not easy. *Tough!* But taxes are harder than Chinese arithmetic.[371] *Sorry, Charlie.*[372] But I hired an accountant who visited China during the 2008 Olympics, and he even had lunch with a renowned Chinese Mathematician to make sure that my taxes were calculated correctly. *No speak English!*

Let's not forget whom we're dealing with . . . "The Original Gangsta." Moreover, let's not be fooled and think that the Matching Game is restricted to W-2s. Old Farmer Joe had a wife named *Old Maid*.

Old Maid is also known as Form 1099. *Old Farmer Joe* and *Old Maid*

---

370 *Spanish* – "It is good" or "that is good"

371 Though I've never tried it, it just seems like something that's overwhelming.

372 "Sorry, Charlie" became closely associated with StarKist Tuna and was a popular American catchphrase. Charlie was a cartoon tuna mascot for StarKist Tuna created by Tom Rogers. Wikipedia, The free encyclopedia Charlie The Tuna (http://en.wikipedia.org/wiki/Sorry_Charlie) (Retrieved 6.24.2010).

got busy and had some kids:

- Miscellaneous Income
- Dividends
- Royalties
- Rents
- Nonemployee Compensation

The matching game is also applicable to their *Cousin Ed*, also known as Form 1098 Mortgage Interest Statements.

The Matching Game is applicable to:

- C Corporations
- S Corporations
- Partnerships
- Limited Liability Companies
- Estates
- Trust
- (No need in beating a dead horse, you get the picture).

I have a good friend who says that tax professionals celebrate Christmas three times a year: April 15th, October 15th, and December 25th. One would think after October 15th, we could take a break and rejuvenate before the new tax season.

Invariably, on October 16th, we encounter a new client who has not filed taxes for over five (5) years. Normally, the client is gripped with fear and is finally ready to face the music. The first thing we do is comfort them; let them know that we will do our absolute best; and they are not alone.

The next thing we do is get the hounds off. We call the Original Gangsta and notify them that we have been hired to represent the client in completing the tax years in question. More importantly, in light of our attempt to become compliant, we ask the Original Gangsta to please refrain from any levy or lien actions.

Prayerfully, the collection specialist agrees and we make one more critical request. "Could you please provide a copy of the income transcript for our Client."

The "income transcript" is nothing more than the score card for "*Old Farmer Joe*." The "income transcript" is to the Original Gangsta what the "Farmer's Almanac" is to "*Old Farmer Joe*." *That is, without it, you're toast!*

The Original Gangsta has a record of every *W-2* and every *Form 1099* that you receive during every tax year. *Every W-2 and 1099?* Yes, every W-2 and Form 1099. Well, actually not every one. *Great Question.* (*Ding, Ding, Ding, Ding*)

As simple and effective as the Matching Game is, *what happens when it don't*[373] *matching?* There are essentially two (2) scenarios that exist when it doesn't match. The first one is . . . . "You Don't Have & They Don't Have."

You Don't Have & They Don't Have

If you don't have an *Old Farmer Joe* (W2) and the Original Gangsta doesn't have an *Old Farmer Joe* (W2), then the story is fairly easy. Most taxpayers will expeditiously call their employer and request a copy of *Old Farmer Joe* as soon as possible in order to ultimately receive their refund.

There are a select few, however, like our friend at the Christmas party, who decided to exclude this income based upon the old principal of, "*it's not what you got, it's what you can prove. I don't have it, you don't have it, and the employer ain't talking. How you like me now!*" (Written with a Kool Mo Dee rhythm in the background).[374]

---

373 "doesn't"
374 Kool Mo Dee is a hip hop MC that was prominent in the late seventies thru eighties, and early nineties. Born August 8, 1962. (Cited at Wikipedia.com (http//en.wikipedia.org/wiki/Kool_Mo_Dee)).

Most of the time, these people get away without paying taxes for years and then, one day, their luck runs out. Trust me, it ain't pretty!

Albeit not often, sometimes the story is flipped;[375] "you have an *Old Farmer Joe*, but they don't."

You Have, But They Don't Have

On occasion, you receive an *Old Farmer Joe* (W2) or *Old Maid* (Form 1099); however, for some strange reason, it doesn't appear on the Farmer's Almanac ("Income Transcript"). Maybe, your employer forgot to mail it; maybe the Original Gangsta lost it (not likely); maybe, there was an agreement to . . . *Never Mind!*

No longer can you mask your "intent" by claiming that you don't have, because you do. "Intent" is a big six letter word, especially when it comes to the law.

Regardless of the situation, "you have and they don't." Well, the options are pretty simple, either you include *Old Farmer Joe* (W2) on your return . . . or you don't. If you include it on your return, the Original Gangsta is grateful. But in a strange psychotic way, don't be surprised if you get audited the very next year.

On the other hand, if you do not include the income on your return, then the complexion of the story changes completely. Normally, the strategy is to exclude *Old Farmer Joe* and/or *Old Maid* from your individual or corporate return; employ the Enron Accounting Paper Shredder Reduction Method; and pray that either the Original Gangsta never discovers the missing document or the employer never provides it.

This move is actually pretty Gangsta in and of itself. Thus leading to the age old question: "What's the difference between tax avoidance and tax evasion?" *About ten (10) years in the federal penitentiary!*

---

375   "Just the opposite"

Intentionally avoiding taxes is a federal offense. [376] If your calling is to break the law, then so be it. As we say in our family *"grown folks doing what grown folks want to do."*

This move is strictly for those who have huge walnuts. Candidly, the decision to exclude an *Old Farmer Joe* (W-2) or *Old Maid* (Form 1099) from the 1040 all comes down to a matter of risk. *How comfortable are you with risk?*

The higher your comfort level, the more likely you are to exclude *Old Farmer Joe* or *Old Maid*. But remember, if the Original Gangsta ever finds out, you could be sharing a 10 x 10 space with a 6 foot 5 inch muscle bound guy named "Rocko" who's holding a mini dress, emphatically stating that it's your size.

Ultimately, if you're willing to take the chance of going to the pokey, then hat's off to you. For those who detest the thought of being told when to sleep, when to eat, and what to eat; and virtually stripped of every human decency that exist, then forego the five hundred and fifty-five dollars ($555.00) of tax savings and include the *Old Farmer Joe* and *Old Maid* on your Form 1040.

Again, my job is not to say "yeah" or "nay." but merely to inform you of the consequences. Make it easy on yourself; call the Original Gangsta; request your income transcript; and insure that all of your information is properly recorded.

The most important factor in this game is knowledge and the application therein. That is, communicating with the Original Gangsta and obtaining a copy of your income transcript is a "good thing." Thereafter, you can play the matching game and make the most informed decision possible. I recommend that you insure that your *Old Farmer Joe* matches the Original Gangsta's *Old Farmer Joe* and your *Old Maid* matches Original Gangsta's *Old Maid*.

Well, now that "we know who our enemy is" and that its gangsta tactics

---

376   *See* "But Paying Taxes Is Unconstitutional", *Supra* cited at Page 49.

are based on nothing more than a mere nursery game, it's time to take the next step.

Prepare For War During A Time Of Peace

The same friend who taught me about "Pay Attention To The Man Behind The Curtain" also taught me to "Prepare For War During A Time of Peace." When I first heard this mantra, I was hooked and started implementing it immediately.

There are a plethora of tax preparers who prepare tax returns, constantly chanting *"I hope they don't audit us, I hope they don't audit us."* Wrong attitude!

Our offensive battle cry is, *"If they audit us, we are prepared for the audit."* Every tax return is prepared with an audit in mind. Does it take more effort? *Yes.* Does it cost more? *Hell yeah.* Will this approach maximize your refund and minimize your tax liability? *Yeah Man!*

Any transaction that has the slightest green hue, thereby yielding tax consequences, must be thoroughly analyzed to determine whether a tax advantage is lurking in the details. With this philosophy in mind, we are positioned to: "Prepare For War During A Time of Peace."

This strategy is a four-step process, consisting of:

1. Praying[377]
2. Thinking Creatively
3. Scribing
4. Praying

If you employ these four steps to your financial and business transactions, you will render unto Caesar that which is Caesar's but nothing more.

---

377   Each step is written in an active sense, because it mandates perpetual activity.

1. PRAYING

The beautiful thing about being a businessman and not a politician is that I "don't have to be politically correct." Every morning when I enter the office, before beginning the day, I begin by audibly reciting the following prayer, entitled "For Your Business:"[378]

> Father, first of all I give You Thanksgiving and praise for blessing me with TaxConcepts[379]. And, as You have given this business unto me, I commit it unto You, and ask for Your blessings upon it.
>
> I pray that You would help me to be faithful in Your work. Help me to be faithful in giving to the Kingdom of God and my service unto You. And, as I am faithful unto You and Your work, I thank You for being faithful to bless and prosper TaxConcepts.
>
> Father, because of my relationship with Christ, and the reflection of Christ upon my life, I pray that You would bless TaxConcepts with a Godly atmosphere, that it may be a reflection of You, and a reflection of Your presence upon it. I pray that every potential customer that comes in contact with me or this business in any way, would sense and feel Your presence, Your peace, Your anointing and Your Spirit.
>
> Your Word says that, if any man lacks wisdom, let him ask of God who liberally gives it to all men and does not hold back. May You give me Your wisdom on how to effectively operate, orchestrate and manage this business, its departments and employees.
>
> Father, I pray for Your favor upon this business and its service. I pray that, by Your Spirit, You would draw in customers from the north, the south, the east and the west. May You draw them from near and far – those who are looking for the products or services

---

378 "For Your Business;" Kenneth Scott, The Weapons Of Our Warfare – Volume Two, Pages 138 -141.

379 The prayer is left blank for each entity to place its name. Every morning we replace the blank "_____" with "TaxConcepts."

of this business. And as people are served and serviced through this business, bless them to continue to do business with us, and tell relatives, friends, neighbors, and acquaintances about this business.

Father, I thank You for a "Spirit of Excellence" in the work, production and service of <u>TaxConcepts</u> to excel in every area. Help me and those that work with me in this business not to be lazy or slothful; but rather, help us to be fervent and diligent in our work.

I pray that You would help me, and every employee or co-worker to work expediently, skillfully, accurately and thoroughly. As we do our work, help us to operate and work in truth, integrity, and honesty. And, as Joseph's work became a testimony to Pharaoh of the Spirit of God in him, I pray that you would likewise bless this business to become a testimony unto You.

I confess Your Word that TaxConcepts is blessed and prosperous in every way and in every area. I confess that <u>TaxConcepts</u> is blessed financially, and blessed continually with financial increase; it is blessed to be a business that lends and not borrows; it is blessed to be the leader in business and not the follower; it is blessed to be above only and not beneath. I thank You that our production is blessed, our income is blessed and our service is blessed. I also confess Your Word that not only is this business blessed, but every employee is blessed exceedingly, abundantly and, above all, in their finances.

By the authority of the name of Jesus Christ, I bind every evil and demonic spirit that would attempt to cause havoc, disruption or hindrance in any way in <u>TaxConcepts</u>. I decree that <u>TaxConcepts</u>, its employees and work area is off limits to every demon and demonic spirit. And I speak the Word of God that no satanic weapon that is formed against this business, employees or co-workers shall be able to prosper or succeed in any way, by the authority of the name of the Lord, Jesus Christ.

Now Father, I commit this business unto You, Your care, and Your direction. And as I have prayed Your Word concerning this business, may You watch over Your Word to perform it, and bring to pass each and everything which I have prayed for and committed to You concerning it.

In the name of Jesus Christ, I pray, AMEN!

Gee Whiz. Long Ain't It! But I know from personal experience prayer works. I come from a praying family and I know the power of prayer. God answer prayers over and over again.

There was a client who recently came to my office with an IRS notice in her hand and fear in her heart. The notice reflected an income omission from her tax return in the amount of sixty-nine thousand, seven hundred and forty-seven thousand dollars ($69,747). The income omission resulted in a tax increase of eleven thousand, three hundred and eighty-five dollars ($11,385).

Since we prepared the return, I was immediately consumed with the notice and began deciphering every letter, comma and period. After reviewing the Notice, it all became clear.

During the applicable tax year, my client received a Form 1099-C (*a.k.a. "Becky," Farmer Joe's Ugly Step Sister*). A Form 1099-C is a method of reporting "cancellation of debt." When I was studying tax law at Howard University School of Law, to say the concept of cancellation of debt was intriguing is a severe understatement. It was one of the most creative thoughts that I had ever heard of in my life.

This is how it works: you have a credit card debt, the creditors have called, but you just don't have the money. After a "reasonable period," the credit card company will write the debt off on their books. *So far, so good.*

The company also sends Becky The Ugly Step-Sister (Form 1099-C) to the IRS. From the Original Gangsta's perspective:

1. At one time, you did indeed owe this debt;
2. You are now relieved of the obligation to pay such debt;
3. Thus, the money that you would have used to pay the debt is now "income" to you and reportable on your Form 1040.
4. *"What you talkin bout Willis?"*[380]

The Original Gangsta is essentially saying that writing the debt off, put money in your pocket so we are gonna[381] be tax it. *"Wait a cotton pickin, dang blasting minute. Writing that debt off didn't put any money in my pocket. I didn't see any increase in my income. No paper, cheddar or scrilla."*

Well unfortunately, the Original Gangsta doesn't see it your way. The cancellation of debt is money in your pocket and the Original Gangsta has the right to get his share.[382]

Back to the story, the IRS said that our client did not include sixty-nine thousand, seven hundred and forty-seven dollars ($69,747) of "cancellation of debt" income and *Tony* is here to collect. After careful review, however, I discovered the aforementioned debt was actually composed of two (2) Form 1099-Cs, each in the exact amount of thirty-four thousand, eight hundred and seventy-three dollars and fifty cents ($34,873.50).

Yureeka, the IRS double counted the credit card debt and you know what . . . we already correctly included the thirty-four thousand, eight hundred and seventy-three dollars and fifty cents ($34,873.50) on the originally submitted Form 1040. *Halleluiah!*

Finding the discrepancy is one thing; proving it to the Original Gangsta is another. *See* "A Conversation with Mrs. Service." During this analytical revelation, our client was gripped with fear and perplexed as to why I was smiling. I explained the discovery and more importantly, I asked everyone in the office to hold hands and we conducted prayer.

---

380 Diff'rent Strokes Television Series. Created by Jeff Harris & Bernie Kukoff. (1978 -1985) NBC; (1985 – 1986) ABC. Quoting Gary Coleman acting as "Arnold Jackson"
381 "are taxing it"
382 There are some exceptions; however, for the most part this is counted as income to be included on your Form 1040.

First, I thanked God for His mercy, love, grace and Son. I asked that we may find favor with Him and favor with the Internal Revenue Service. I specifically asked that the Internal Revenue Service recognize its mistake and correct it immediately. I sealed it in love, faith and abundant praise. Amen.

After calling the IRS, we spoke with the most accommodating representative and the matter was zealously resolved. Our client's tax liability went from eleven thousand, three hundred and eighty-five dollars ($11,385.00) to zero, nada, zilch in a matter of seventeen (17) minutes flat.

Out client was extremely happy. We have provided great service; moreover, the tremendous tax savings was an incentive for prompt payment; not to mention, the greatest advertisement we could ever obtain.

The real question is again, what about the *"Man behind the curtain?"* How many taxpayers have received the same letter, panicked, and/or had inadequate counsel and pleaded to the Original Gangsta for an installment agreement in an effort to *"leave me alone, just leave me alone."*

I believe in prayer and I've personally witnessed and experienced God's miracles. Many people believe a miracle can only occur if the Red Sea parts or water is turned into wine (*and I'm told that it was good wine*)[383]. I submit, however, that miracles occur whenever someone emphatically states that, "it can not be done and God intervenes to show He is the ultimate decision maker for all that we can possibly imagine.

Incredibly, what was undeniably "no" miraculously became "yes." A manager suddenly changes her mind; or the obstinate agent that was so uncooperative is absent from work due to sickness and the manager steps in and graciously approves that loan; or any other time that God shows up right on time.

---

383 *See* John 2:1-11, Cana Wedding Miracle. http://bibleresources.bible.com (Retrieved 3.29.10).

Prayer is a good thing. I like to pray in our office, but I also like to pray in the venue where I'm appearing. I ask God to give me wisdom and knowledge; hear the words that He would have me hear; speak the words that He would have me speak, and whatever the result, I thank Him for His grace and I will continue to give Him all of the honor, glory and praise.

Prayer works. This is the first step to "Preparing For War During A Time of Peace."

2. THINKING CREATIVELY

Thinking Creatively is a vital component of "Preparing For War During A Time Of Peace." Why wait until a challenge is imminent when we can use a little gray matter between our ears and factually anticipate possible outcomes? It's practical! It's strategic! It's great offense!

My good friends, *creative thinking is not in the "taking of deductions;" it's in the "making of deductions."* Let me repeat . . . *creative thinking is not in the "taking," but in the "making."*

In tax, the answer is not as important as the analysis; that is, how was the answer reached. In other words, if you can get the right people to understand why your answer is correct, the process will yield the same results time after time. Thus, the answer is irrelevant, but the creative process is key!

Thinking creatively requires a fresh mind and can magically transform a personal debt into an expense. *Wait a minute. Isn't that what I pay my accountant or tax attorney to do? It's their job to think creatively and tell me how much I owe at the end of the year.* Actually, that's only part of the job. No one knows more or has more control over your daily actions than you.

The challenge with thinking creatively is that it mandates going up to the line, touching it; looking over it (just to see where not to go or how to evade it); and stretching it if necessary. As attorneys, we are trained

to not only push the line, but also bend it, mangle it, or even make it magically disappear; however, under no circumstances should we break it.

When a tax return or transaction is close to the line, we inform our clients that we're close to the line. We inform the client of the consequences, and let them make the decision. That way, we can sleep soundly at night.

I still don't get it. How does one think creatively about tax? Or as my son, says "example please."

The Robinson Vacation

Once upon a time, there was the Robinson family of three traveling to Disney for spring break. Mr. Robinson was a computer analyst; Mrs. Robinson was an attorney; and Baby Robinson was 7 years old.

Normally, this family would, at a minimum incur the following expenses:

- Airfare
- Lodging
- Meals and
- Ground Transportation

Certainly, these expenses are personal in nature and can not possibly be categorized as a deduction. *"Or can they?"*

Approximately one week before the Robinsons left for their vacation, Mr. Robinson called an Orlando computer firm and requested the opportunity to drop off his resume. Mrs. Robinson followed suit and left her resume with an Orlando law firm. The employers are governed by

the Fair Employment Act,[384] so they welcomed the resumes with open arms.[385]

The Robinsons also requested a business card from the human resource department manager or managing partner. *Why?* Remember we're still preparing for war. It's not what is; it's what you can prove.[386]

What's more, the computer firm and the law firm should send a letter, informing the Robinson that "in spite of your outstanding abilities, credentials, experience and exposure, we are unable to accommodate your request for a position with our firm."

That's okay. I never wanted that stinkin job anyway. Even though the grapes were probably sour,[387] you have a record, verifying your job seeking expenses. If you get the job, then it's a wonderful thing to have more than you truly need. If you don't get the job, then you're still entitled to deduct the expenses as a job seeking expense.

Job seeking expenses? Yes job seeking expenses. If you are looking for a new job in your present occupation and you incur expenses, then you may be able to deduct those expenses on your Schedule "A" "Itemized Deductions."[388] More importantly, you can claim these expenses as a deduction "even if you don't get the job."[389] *Even if you don't get the job?*

---

384   Executive Order 8802 signed by President Franklin D. Roosevelt on June 25, 1941, was the first federal law to promote equal opportunity and prohibit employment discrimination in the United States. The executive order was issued in response to pressure from civil rights activist Bayard Rustin, A. Philip Randolph, and A. J. Muste who had planned a march on Washington, D.C. to protest racial discrimination. The march was suspended after Executive Order 8802 was issued. Executive Order 8802 – Wikipedia, the free encyclopedia; http://en.wikipedia.org/wiki/Fair_Employment_Act (Retrieved 01.18.2010) (citing Roy L. Brooks, et al. Civil Rights Litigation: Cases and Perspectives, 2nd ed. Pages 398-99. Carolina Academic Press 2000.

385   Note: Mr. and Mrs. Robinson must have the sincere intent to pursue the job.

386   Infra "Scribing."

387   *See* Internal Revenue Code §67; Treas. Regs. 1.67-1T2(a)(1)(i).; and Internal Revenue Service, Publication 529, page 5. Note: You cannot deduct these expenses if: 1) you are looking for a job in a new occupation, 2) there was a substantial break between the ending of your last job and you are looking for a new one, or 3) you are looking for a job for the first time.

388   Internal Revenue Service, Publication 529, page 5. Note: You cannot deduct these expenses if: 1) you are looking for a job in a new occupation, 2) there was a substantial break between the ending of your last job and your looking for a new one, or 3) you are looking for a job for the first time.

389   *Id.*

That's right, even if you don't get the job.

Well, what kinda of expenses are you talking about? What about if you:

- *travel for an interview;*
- *hire a resume preparation firm or an employment agency;*
- *legal fees related to doing or keeping your job?*[390]

Yep. You got it. All of these expenses are deductible as "job seeking expenses."

By thinking creatively and preparing in advance, you have magically transformed a personal expense into an itemized deduction. You can deduct a portion of the airfare, lodging, meal and ground transportation expenses.

Caution: Don't get greedy and claim Baby Robinson's toys purchased at Disney nor the park tickets and don't claim all seven (7) days of meals and lodging. Formulate a reasonable amount that can be substantiated before the Original Gangsta in the event of an audit. *This is how we think creatively.*

Can you give me another example of *"thinking creatively."* Sure.

<u>Sister Jones</u>

Once upon a time, God made a happy tax attorney leave his good New York managerial job with Ernst & Young and start his own business (*See* Genesis). *Sniff, Sniff.*

Because he believed in and liked the blessings of tithing, he tithed his services at the Mothership Church of God. As a part of tithing his services, he decided to provide free individual tax preparation to anyone who tithed their money to the church and earned less than forty thousand dollars ($40,000).

---

390 *Id.*

Sister Jones was a tithing member of the Mothership Church and appropriately scheduled an appointment to have her tax return completed. Sister Jones was a single parent and worked at Henry Medical Hospital. She sang soprano in the choir; had practice twice a week; and sang in three (3) services each Sunday. As the tax attorney was mentally calculating Sister Jones' return, he was confronted with a new situation relating to charitable contributions.

Background. If one volunteers their services to a charitable organization, then contrary to popular belief, the fair market value of such services are not deductible.[391]

From a policy stand point, service valuations are a credibility and valuation nightmare. That is, how does one truly value the worth of his services? More importantly, how will the Original Gangsta monitor and insure that the proper value is deducted. If you think about it, there is no way the Original Gangsta would allow you to deduct the fair market value of your services.

Although all of those reading this book are upstanding law abiding citizens, there are some who prefer to give in to "the dark side."[392] Somewhere, Darth Vader is saying, *"You see although my salary is fifty thousand dollars ($50,000), my true net valuable of my services is five hundred thousand ($500,000). Based upon the raise the Emperor Sidious[393] is going to give me calculated at future value for twenty-five years . . . yeah, yeah, yeah!*

The Original Gangsta is completely unwilling to take this chance. Although you are unable to deduct the fair market value of your services, you can deduct any out of pocket expenses including mileage.[394]

---

391 *See* Treas. Regs. 1.170-2(a)(2) and Internal Revenue Service Publication 526 "Charitable Contributions" Page 5, CAT. No. 15050A (Revised December 16, 2009).

392 "Star Wars." Created by George Lucas. Released May 25, 1977 by Century Fox. Star Wars – The Wikipedia, The Free Encyclopedia (Retrieved May 26, 2010).

393 *Id.*

394 *See* Internal Revenue Code §162 and Treas. Regs. 1.162

Thanks for the background, but how does this apply to Sister Jones? This is where we must employ the creative thinking.

As the tax attorney was listening to Sister Jones, his tax radar senses clicked and he distinctly remembered her stating that she was a choir member and attended choir practice at least three times a week.

Bingo, Bango, Bongo. The Church is an IRC Sec. 501(c)(3) organization; hence, some of Sister Jones choir activities should be deductible. Sister Jones can deduct the mileage to and from the Mothership's choir practice. *Cool. Cool. Cool.*

Note, the creative analysis is not only in the recognition, but the application. The Mothership Church of God has three (3) Sunday Services[395]: 8:00, 10:00, and 12:00. The choir sings at all three services. *Then it hit him like a proverbial rock.* Being the faithful member that she is, Sister Jones enjoyed hearing the Good Reverend Right preach the word. Since there are three services, it was determined that Sister Jones attended one service for her religious edification and the remaining two services she was volunteering her services as a choir member.

Given that Sister Jones is volunteering her services for two out of three services, then she should be able to deduct two-thirds (2/3) of the mileage to and from her home on Sunday morning. We can also deduct her robe purchasing expenses, robe cleaning expenses and the patent leather shoes that she purchased. *Not bad. Not bad. Hey, what about "uniform expenses?"*

Uniform Expenses

As an attorney I am required to wear a suit everyday and continuous inappropriate dress could lead to grounds for contempt of court. In spite of this clothing mandate, I do not satisfy the uniform deduction requirement.

---

395 Intentionally capitalized for inflection.

You can claim your clothes as a uniform deduction, only if two (2) requirements are satisfied:

1. You must wear them as a condition of your employment and
2. The clothes are not suitable for everyday wear.[396]

Well hell, how many of us can actually qualify for the uniform deduction and why did they make it so darn hard? Who Can?

- Delivery workers (UPS/FedEx);
- Firefighters;
- Health Care Workers;
- Law Enforcement Officers;
- Letter Carriers;
- Professional Athletes[397]
- Transportation Workers (Air, Rail, Bus.)
- Even Musicians and Entertainers may deduct the cost of theatrical clothing and accessories that are not suitable for everyday wear.[398]

Why them and not me? Too many people would utilize the deduction which would ultimately reduce the treasury. "Reducing the treasury" is contrary to the Original Gangsta's mission - *collect the paper, not give it away.*

Note: Even though painters wear white caps, white shirts or jackets, white bib overalls and standard union required work shoes, such clothing is not distinctive in nature to qualify as a uniform.[399]

What had happen[400] with the white thing?[401] Some union guy made

---

396   Internal Revenue Service, Publication 529 Page 7.
397   Get real! Professional athletes do not wash their uniforms. I have no idea why the IRS made this recommendation.
398   *See* Treas. Reg. 1.67-1T2(a)(i) and Publication 529 at page 8.
399   *Id.*
400   "happened"
401   This has got to be one of the few exceptions where being white is not a good thing.

some Senator real upset over a bad paint job. Who Knows?

The real question is how do we turn a painter's uniform into a deductible expense? Certainly, we could change the uniform color, but that's too easy. What about changing the uniform color and adding a company logo? What about changing the uniform color, adding a company logo; and monogramming the painter's name on the uniform in the company's official colors? *Now, we got a shot!*

Thinking creatively is merely paying attention to our lifestyle and analyzing how we can possibly transform our daily events into a legitimate tax deduction. Consider this:

- We wake up in the morning and take a shower. Did we take advantage of that special water heater that provides a tax credit?
- We attended dinner with friends. During the meeting you discuss forming a real estate investment trust (REIT). After paying for the bill, on the back of the receipt you write: who attended the meeting and the general discussion topic. *Meals and Entertainment Expense?*
- You are a realtor looking for properties, are you recording your mileage in your log book. *Transportation Expenses?*

With everything you do, ask yourself, "*is this a taxable deduction or expense?*" More importantly, if this is not a taxable deduction or expense, how can you legitimately and magically "transform" it into a taxable deduction or expense?

Thinking creatively is in the details. Note: It is only beneficial if:

1. Your tax professional is capable, willing and competent; and
2. You communicate these transactions to such professional.

At TaxConcepts, our clients call us, describing innumerable situations and inquiring about the possible tax consequences or benefits. One hundred percent of the time our answers fall into one of three categories: "*Yes,*" "*No,*" or "*We don't know, we'll research it, analyze the*

possibilities, and get back with you."

During the course of each day, we encounter good and challenging circumstances. The questions are "how do we approach the situation" and "what is our attitude?"

I submit that approaching the situation initially from a position of gratitude that God gave us another day to get it right releases the creative juices. By allowing our minds to flow, we can see and appreciate circumstances from a completely different perspective.

It's a wonderful thing! When we approach our daily lives with the right frame of reference, then we can develop the proper attitude, not only to succeed, but to excel. Attitude, properly executed, will take you places your body didn't know it could go.

When your approach is right, then your attitude is right. When your attitude is right, your mind is right. Everything else is just paper work and prayer. Because at the end of the day, it's all good and it's all God. I encourage you to think creatively and reap the spiritual and financial rewards.

3. SCRIBE

To paraphrase my cousin, if wisdom is indicative of brevity, then this is the wisest subchapter of them all. Believe it or not, the hard part is done.

Scribe n. –

1. a person who serves as a professional copyist, especially one who made copies of manuscripts before the invention of printing.
2. a public clerk or writer, usually one having official status. .
3. Also called sopher, sofer. Judaism. One of the group of Palestinian scholars and teachers of Jewish law and tradition, active from the 5th century *B.C.* to the 1st century *A.D.*, who

transcribed, edited, and interpreted the Bible.[402]

Even though the hard part (thinking creatively and creating the deduction) has already been done, if we don't do the paper work, then all of our efforts are in vain. Preparing For War During A Time of Peace requires that we serve as scribes in order to record and categorize our receipts, logs and records. *Dude, do you know how hard it is for me to keep up with paper work? It's just not my thing.*

Correction, *"it wasn't your thing."* In "Preparing For War During a Time of Peace," the war is the audit. If you ever, and I pray that it doesn't happen, receive a certified letter from the IRS, then you will wish that paperwork had been *"your thing."*

My good friends, tax audit representation is what I do for a living. During the audit, what happened in the year in question is irrelevant. The real question is *"What can you prove?"*

When dealing with the Original Gangsta, "your only proof is documentation." During an audit, you must provide receipts, logs, and other substantiating documents.

Trust me, there is no throwing yourself on the mercy of the Original Gangsta's court. Few of us have neither the income nor the time to contest a matter in tax court; so, for most practical purposes, there is no court. The revenue agent serves as the judge, jury, opposing counsel and bailiff. *Welcome to my world!*

Before an audit, my client check list includes:

1. Categorizing receipts and making sure that each one answers the pertinent questions of who, what, when, and why.
2. Making sure that the logs are properly recorded, bound, and each exhibit is properly identified.
3. Meeting the auditor on our turf. Most auditors don't like to stay in the office and its always fundamental military strategy to fight

---

402   *See* www.Dictionary.com

the war on the most familiar terrain. So, the auditor is in our plush conference room, unlike the sterile digs of the Feds, and we are providing water, coffee, tea, and light snacks at his/her every request.

Now that the stage is set, let the fun begin. While representing our client, we defer to the auditor respectfully, while simultaneously relentlessly defending our client.

After an initial interview with our client, the auditor will normally begin by inquiring about a particular expense. Let's say that the auditor is curious about the "meals and entertainment expenses" and request to see those receipts.

- First, we examine the return to confirm the amount claimed.
- Second, we examine the QuickBooks Income and Expense Worksheet we created and provided to the auditor.
- Finally, we present the auditor with the receipts from the neatly stacked categorized pile.

Next, the auditor asks about the "car and truck expenses." Again, we examine the tax return to confirm the amount claimed; we examine the QuickBooks Income and Expense Worksheet; and finally, we provide the travel mileage log for confirmation. Normally, after going through this process, back and forth, a rapport is eventually established and the auditor is grateful for the presentation of records in such an orderly fashion. Meticulous presentation minimizes our client's tax liabilities and efficiently maximizes their retainer fee.

This fantastic representation and reduction in tax liability was successful because the "The Scribe" a.k.a., "you" provided us with the evidence to prove your case. Truth be told, scribing is not that difficult. All you have to do is keep your receipts, categorize them accordingly, and record your mileage in the neat log book that is kept in the glove compartment. That's all.

You see, tax representation is at its best when we work hand in hand with our client. Moral of the Story: "If you don't have the paper to back up a deductible activity, as far as the Original Gangsta is concerned . . . it never happened." *Coppice? Coppice!*

4. PRAY

When I was growing up, I was taught not to refuse several things. Prayer was one of them. After completing a tax return, we always pray over the documents prior to filing.

We ask God to bless and anoint the return. We ask that if anyone is not saved,[403] that they will merely look at the return and notice that something is different and be lead to Jesus Christ.

We further pray that the Internal Revenue Service process the return in an effective, efficient and expedient manner. We thank God for His grace, mercy and love. And we thank Him for His blessings. In Jesus name. Amen.

Why? After analyzing the return, researching the law, and preparing the return, we pray primarily because, *"it sure can't hurt."* After our absolute professional best, there is nothing else we can do and prayer seals the deal.

Many of our clients are not Christians; however, interestingly enough, not once has anyone said, *"Stop that Jesus praying, you Bible-toting, tongue-confessing, Church-going Christian."* Clients merely say, "Amen," pay their invoice and keep rolling.

Not only do we pray after completing returns, but we also pray before audits, examinations, and installment agreement request. We also pray over every document that is produced and submitted to Secretary of States, State Revenue Departments, and any other tax-related document that is produced, analyzed or distributed.
Recently, I remember one situation in particular. As we already know,

---

403   Romans 10:9. KJV.

the Original Gangsta is socially driven and, during a recession, more innovative and expeditious methods are implemented to collect federal taxes. I discovered, that the Original Gangsta had taken its collection activity to another level. Kicked it up a notch, as one would say.[404]

One afternoon, a new client called and needed assistance immediately. After meeting with him and reviewing his papers, I was flabbergasted. My new client had submitted an amended return that resulted in a reduction of income in excess of one hundred thousand dollars ($100,000.00). Not to our surprise, the return was audited.

The Original Gangsta, however, did not send the typical CP 2000 letter, explaining the discrepancies and giving the taxpayer an opportunity to "agree," "disagree," or "partially agree." This time the Original Gangsta mailed a letter, stating:

We are examining the amended return and we will be at your home on: Jan. x, 20xx, Monday at 10:00 a.m. The attached list describes in detail the information we're going to need.

And by the way, although it's never mentioned, we're also going to evaluate your home and life style to see if there are any taxable transactions that you may have intentionally or unintentionally overlooked.

Unfortunately, my client did not receive the letter. One fine Monday morning after eating breakfast and kissing his wife and son goodbye, the door bell rang. Original Gangsta, Revenue Agent Thomas was at the door and she's holding a computer, several files, a cell phone, and an adding machine with tape. All government standard issued.

Although I maintain every morning is a good morning, after learning about this client, we can all probably agree certainly there are some days that are better than others. Our client informed Revenue Agent Thomas that he was unaware of the audit and it was impossible to continue.

---

404   A saying by Emeril John Lagasse, (Born October 15, 1959 -)*See* http://en.wikipedia.org/wiki/ Emeril_Lagasse. (Retrieved 3.15.2012).

Furthermore, he stated that he would hire proper counsel and contact her within twenty-four (24) hours.

Selah.[405] This client chose wisely. Yet, let us consider all of those who, confronted with the same circumstances, would have permitted the audit to continue due to fear and intimidation. Thank God for this client's discernment.

By Monday afternoon, we were retained and we immediately left a message with Agent Thomas. We called again on Tuesday, Wednesday, and Thursday.

Friday morning, we decided to give it another try. I had not prayed, because I was just making an introduction. *Dumb! Dumb! Dumb!* In all things acknowledge me and I will direct thy path.[406] All things mean "all things".

"Agent Thomas, this is Aislee Smith. I'm with TaxConcepts and we represent Client. We left you several messages; however, I was unable to contact you."

"I got your messages. However, since I didn't see Client on Monday at 10:00, then my manager, Mrs. Rivers recommended closing your case and it is not open to review. So, your client hired you just a little too late."

As Agent Thomas was hanging the phone up, I could hear her snickering in the background. Upon hearing the wonderful news, I was floored. Everyone makes mistakes and now our client has hired counsel to resolve the tax discrepancy. *"Trust me,"* if I didn't know I needed to pray before the call, I definitely knew I had to pray now.
In spite of the news, I kept my cool. I asked Agent Thomas if she would please provide me with the correct spelling of Mrs. Rivers' name and telephone number. After scribing the information, I began to pray:

---

405 *See* Selah, *Supra* cited at Footnote 41.
406 Proverbs 3:6. KJV.

"Dear God, we ask for favor with You and the Internal Revenue Service. We pray that You touch Mrs. Rivers' heart and let her miraculously change her mind. Father, all we ask is for the opportunity to present our case and we will follow your word. Upon receiving the victory, we will give you all of the honor, glory, and praise. In the precious name of your Son Jesus we pray. Amen"

"Mrs. Rivers?"

"Yes"

"This is Aislee Smith and we're calling regarding Client. We would appreciate it greatly if you could give us the opportunity to present the appropriate tax records.

"Hold on. Can you meet on the 14th of February?"

"Yes Ma'am, we'll call on the 13th to confirm. Thank you for your assistance."

Thank you God. We give You all the honor, praise, and glory. Halleluiah! Fifteen minutes later, Revenue Agent Thomas called and confirmed the meeting of the 14th. After exchanging pleasantries and confirming the appointment, Agent Thomas said, "what did you say to my manager? I've been at the IRS for over eleven years and she never changes her mind."

With a smile across my face, I politely told Agent Thomas the only thing we did was pray before calling. Agent Thomas was overwhelmed. More so, when we met, the foundation was already laid and the examination went extremely well. Client actually received an additional refund as a result of the audit. Amen. Ain't Jesus so gud![407]

However, I can't take the credit for thinking to praying. Mightier men than me have prayed for far greater things. These men of God have set

---

407 "good"

the standard and showed us how, with God, we can accomplish anything regardless of the odds. *I know, I know, you're still not convinced.* Well let me tell you about a story of "One Against Many" and the Power of Prayer.

One Against Many

Once upon a time there was a mean lady named Jezebel. Jezebel's heart was ten times smaller than the "Grinch Who Stole Christmas" heart.[408] I can hear my son actually having pity for her, because she was so mean it was apparent that she didn't grow up with a Mommy or Daddy.

To this day, Jezebel's name is associated with vile, devious, and murderous actions. Jezebel prayed to a god named "Baal." Naturally, Jezebel was able to obtain cohorts through her manipulative nature and one of her main captains was Ahab. Of course, it follows if Jezebel was mean as a snake, then in order to find favor in her army; you had to be equally as nasty.

Jezebel and Ahab woke up every morning with evil on their minds. Each waking moment was consumed with feverously attempting to think of devious ways to separate the children of Israel from their God. I'm not too sure who said it, but I once heard, "If you say a lie loud enough and long enough, eventually someone will believe it."

Such was the case in these times. In spite of the fact that, God is a jealous God and thou shall have none before Him,[409] the Israelites began to waiver in their faith. *Oh, Oh, I can smell a rumble in the mix.*

One morning, God gave a message to one of his favorite prophets, Elijah.[410] During this time, there was a drought and God let Elijah know it was time to do what He does.

---

408 *See* "How the Grinch Stole Christmas," Written by Dr. Seuss. Published in November 24, 1957 by OCLC Number 178325. Random House.
409 Deuteronomy 5:7 & 9.
410 1 Kings 18:1. NRS.

God told Elijah to present himself to Ahab for the battle royal of all time. We gonna rumble, we gonna rumble tonighttttt! (Written in a "West Side Story" Puerto Rican accent.)[411] This battle royal will determine who is for God and who is for Baal.

As soon as Ahab saw Elijah he exclaimed, "there you are, you troublemaker of Israel, you are responsible for bringing this drought upon us."[412] Elijah responded, "No Ahab, it is you who is responsible for the drought on the land. You and your father have disobeyed the Lord and chosen to follow Baal instead.[413] Now, it's time for the battle royal. Go gather all of the Israelites, the four hundred (400) prophets of Baal and the four hundred and fifty (450) Asherah prophets who eat at Jezebel's table and let's get it on. Meet me at Mount Carmel tomorrow morning and don't be late![414]

Wow, that's what you gotta love about people like Elijah. When God gives them a command, they just get up and do it. There is no debate or *"God, are you sure this is what you want me do" or "God, can you send me another sign?"*[415] When Elijah received the command, he got up and handled God's business.

Wait a minute, Elijah handling God's business meant one man with the backing of God going up against a plethora of Asherah prophets. Not to mention, the Israelites who were wavering in their faith. Nonetheless, Elijah did his thing with unabashed faith and persistence.
Later on, the newsflash hit the streets: *"Hurry, Hurry, Read All About It . . . Greatest fight since David and Goliath*[416]*. . . Elijah, Man of God going up against Baal's thousand . . . be there or be square. Don't miss it."*

---

411   West Side Story. Written by Arthur Laurents. Music by Leonard Bernstein and lyrics by Stephen Sondheim. Based on William Shakespeare's Romeo and Juliet. Distributed by United Artist on October 18, 1961. Citing Wikipedia, the free encyclopedia (West Side Story (film) – Wikipedia, the free encyclopedia) (http://enwikipedia.org/wiki/West_Side_Story (film). (Retrieved May 26, 2010)

412   1 Kings 18:17. NRS.

413   1 Kings 18:18. NRS.

414   1 Kings 18:19. NRS.

415   There was this Gideon testing the Lord with the fleece thing; however that was "special." Only God and Gideon know for sure. *See* Judges 6:36 King James Version

416   1 Samuel 17 NRS.

Somewhere around the corner, a scalper was lurking and whispering, *"Hey man, let me talk to you for a quick second."* (**Warning Will Robinson, Warning!**)[417] "I got two tickets left to the fight, and they're worth twenty-five (25) drekels. Because I know you really want to go the event, I'm gonna sell them to you at a deal. For this one time only, you can get the tickets for ten (10) drekels and the ticket has the commemorative Mount Carmel symbol as a reminder that you were there at the big fight."

Everything works out well, until you get to the fight and find out that the entry fee is only five (5) drekels and "cash only."

"But I got a ticket that I purchased for ten (10) drekels." Sorry Pal, "cash only." *"But it has the Mount Carmel commemorative stamp."* "Fork up the five (5) drekels or get out the line!" *But. But.* Security! **Lesson Learned**.

The next morning, the show down began between Elijah, Man of God vs. The Prophets of Baal with the Children of Israel caught in the middle. Before the fight, Elijah gave the Israelites a great opportunity. Elijah gave them a chance to choose God before the fight began.

Elijah said, "How long will you go lingering with two different opinions. If the Lord is God, follow Him, but if Baal is God, then follow him."[418]

Essentially, this was a faith opportunity. Faith is the "substance of things hoped for and the evidence of things unseen."[419]

What is this evidence of things unseen? Unseen is victory despite what you see. *Well, I see a whole lot of people getting ready to mop the floor up with poor old Elijah, and back in those days, they had dirt floors.* Yet, I submit that, if you make the choice to follow God under these insurmountable circumstances, God will bless you even more

---

417 Lost In Space. Science fiction television series created by Irwin Allen (1965 – 1968). Note: First season shot in black and white; remaining seasonings filmed in color. "Daddy, what is black and white?
418 1 Kings 18:21. NRS.
419 Hebrews 11:1. NRS.

abundantly, just because you believed!

Alas, such was not the case in this heated battle. When Elijah gave the Children of Israel the faith opportunity, they were completely silent.[420] One thing I gotta give the Israelites credit for, although they didn't say that they were for God, in their silence they didn't say that they were against Him.

Elijah continued with his mandate and, when you're walking with God, you can step boldly. And Elijah did indeed step bad. At the Battle Royal, Elijah challenged the prophets of Baal to a contest. Elijah told the people to bring two bulls for a sacrifice.[421] After choosing one bull each,[422] both contenders were told to cut his bull into pieces and place it on the wood on the alter.[423] But here's the tricky part, they were told not to put any fire near the sacrifice.[424] You call on your god and I'll call on my God.[425] The first God that sets the wood on fire is the "winner, winner chicken dinner."[426]

Elijah then told Baal and his crew, "my God is so bad, I will let you choose first. Which bull do you want?[427] It don't[428] make a difference I'm gonna win anyway." After a lengthy discussion, the Baal crew chose the bull on the right.

---

420   1 Kings 18:21. NRS.

421   1 Kings 18:23. NRS.

422   Perhaps the bulls were used because it's said that these animals are stubborn in nature and so far the children of Israel ain't budging.

423   1 Kings 18:23. NRS.

424   *Id.*

425   1 Kings 18:24. NRS.

426   Randy Pedersen (born 1962) is a professional bowler and color analyst of ESPN's Professional Bowling Association (PBA) tour. As a bowler, Randy won 13 PBA titles (including the prestigious PBA National Championship crown in 1987) and retired as the 24th millionaire in PBA history. As an analyst, Pedersen created several "Randy-ism including "Winner, winner, Chicken dinner!" (Referring to the winner of a match). Citing Wikipedia, the Free encyclopedia (Randy-Wikipedia, the free encyclopedia) (http://en.wikipedia.org/wiki/Randy_Pedersen) (Retrieved May 26, 2010). Also quoted in "Jerry Maguire," Written and directed by Cameron Crowe; Produced by: James L. Brooks, Cameron Crowe, Laurence Mark and Richard Sakai. Studio Gracie Films. Distributed by TriStar Pictures. Release date December 13, 1996. Citing Wikipedia, the free encyclopedia. (Jerry Maguire – Wikipedia, the free encyclopedia) (http://en.wikipedia.org/wiki/Jerry_McGuire) (Retrieved May 26, 2010).

427   1 Kings 18:25. NRS.

428   "doesn't"

During the time, I'm sure that the Baal prophets were thinking, *"Sucker, we gonna beat you like an egg getting ready for some Jiffy cornbread."* Can you imagine the odds on the fight? Somewhere in the crowd, our friend who purchased the ticket still hasn't learned his lesson.

"Taking all bets, taking all bets"

"Excellent idea, I'll take my last drekel and bet on the Baal crew. At least I can get some of my money back from the whack[429] ticket deal and see a good whipping in the process."

Meanwhile, Elijah was just laying in the *cut*.[430] So, the Baal crew prepared the bull and put it on the alter.[431] Then they called on Baal's name from morning to the afternoon.[432] "O Baal, answer us" and much like the children of Israel, there was no reply.[433] They called and they prayed, they sang and they dance, but nothing happen. Not one single solitary spark was ignited to consume the alter. Although it's rumored that a suggestion was made to get a piece of flint to try and ignite . . . Hhmmm.

Meanwhile, Elijah began mocking the Baal crew. "Cry aloud. Surely, he is a god. Either he is meditating or he has wandered away, or he is on a journey, or perhaps he is asleep and must be awakened."[434] The Baal crew continued their worship service and they even began the ritual order of cutting themselves with knives and swords until blood began to gush.[435] All this in the name of their Baal god to show up. Nonetheless, Baal was a no show. All day, hour after hour, the Baal prophets called upon their god and, by the evening, they gave up.[436]

Somewhere in the crowd, the guy who purchased the ticket from the scalper is saying: *"You mean to tell me that I gambled my last drekel for*

---

429 "illegitimate"
430 Waiting patiently and meditatively until its time to execute the plan.
431 1 Kings 18:26. NRS.
432 *Id.*
433 *Id.*
434 1 Kings 18:27. NRS.
435 1 Kings 18:28. NRS.
436 1 Kings 18:29. NRS.

a fight and it's a no show. You gotta be kidding me!"

Needless to say, the brother had no idea what he was in for. When God shows up, He shows up. God can't help but to show out, because He's God all by Himself.

At the usual time for the evening sacrifice, Elijah called the people closer and gathered twelve (12) stones.[437] A stone was gathered for each of Israel tribes and he repaired the alter in the name of the Lord.[438]

Then he told the people to dig a large trench around the alter.[439] Next, he placed the wood on the alter, cut the bull in pieces, and laid it on the wood.[440] Then he told the people to fill four large jars with water and pour the water over the offering and the wood.[441] Do it again! Do it again! Do it again![442] There was so much water that it ran off the sacrifice and filled the trench.[443]

Do you think maybe God was trying to send a message! "Do it again," so that when He shows up, you will have no doubt that He and He alone is God.

After drenching the bull sacrifice with water like a piece of fried chicken baptized in hot grease, Elijah prayed, I repeat Elijah prayed:

"O Lord, God of Abraham, Isaac, and Israel, let it be known that this day that you are God of Israel, that I am your servant, and that I have done all these things at your bidding. Answer me, O Lord, answer me, so that these people may know that you, O Lord, are God, and that you have turned their hearts back."[444]

Immediately upon finishing his prayer, the fire of the Lord came down;

---

437 1 Kings 18:31. NRS.
438 *Id.*
439 1 Kings 18:32. NRS.
440 1 Kings 18:33. NRS.
441 *Id.*
442 1 Kings 18:34. NRS.
443 1 Kings 18:835. NRS.
444 1 Kings 18:36. NRS.

consumed the burnt offering, the wood, the stones, and the dust; and even licked up the water that was in the trench.[445] When the people saw it, they fell down on their faces and said, "The Lord indeed is God; the Lord indeed is God."[446] *No freaking kidding!*

You've just seen one of the greatest shows of all time and all of a sudden "God is indeed God." Well, thank God for His grace, because none of us are perfect.

But does it really take all of that to show that He is indeed God? Wasn't this the same God that parted the Red Sea;[447] wasn't this the same God that destroyed the world with water, except for a few survivors on Noah's ark;[448] wasn't this the same God that delivered you from the hands of Pharaoh and brought you to the promise land, flowing with milk & honey?[449]

It's all a matter of what you believe. The Bible says, "if you have the faith of a mustard seed and say to the mountain be moved and it shall be moved and nothing shall be impossible to you."[450] Last time I checked, a mustard seed is about the size of the top of a stick pin. Apparently, Elijah must have had such faith, because he was faced with undefeatable odds. Yet, despite these odds, his prayer was simple.

"O Lord, God of Abraham, Isaac, and Israel, let it be known that this day that you are God in Israel, that I am your servant, and that I have done all these things at your bidding. Answer me, O Lord, answer me, so that these people may know that you, O Lord, are God, and that you have turned their hearts back."[451]

I've always heard that the God we praise is the same God that Elijah and all of the other prophets praised. Thus, when confronted with challenges

---

445 1 Kings 18:38. NRS.
446 1 Kings 18:39. NRS.
447 *See.* Exodus 12:17 – 15:21. NRS
448 *See.* Genesis 6 -9. NRS
449 *See.* Exodus 3:8. NRS.
450 Matthew 17:20 King James Version.
451 *Id.* at 36.

far less than the Mount Carmel Battle Royal, I recommend prayer.

Certainly, an audit with the Original Gangsta does not compare to turning your heart against God (or at least I don't think it does). So, if God can consume the sacrifice, wood, and water, surely he can assist in dealing with the Internal Revenue Service. Moreover, as mentioned earlier, it sure can't hurt.

Wait a minute, what happen to the Baal prophets? Elijah told the people to, *"Seize the Baal crew and bring them down to the Kishon Brook and kill them all."*[452]

Review

Preparing for war during a time of peace is a four (4) step process:

1. Praying
2. Thinking Creatively
3. Scribing
4. Praying

If you employ this process, you will "Render unto Caesar . . . But Nothing More." More importantly, you are positioning yourself for a battle royal with the Original Gangsta in the event that it should occur. And if the battle never occurs, then it sure doesn't hurt to be prepared.

I assure you, if you "Get your Mind Right" and combine these principles with "Tithing From a Tax Perspective," then you will:

1. Increase Your Refund Or Reduce Your Liability Tremendously.
2. Reduce the Chance Of Being Audited.
3. Satisfy Your Legal Tax Responsibilities
4. Get Blessed in the Process.

Get Your Mind Right!

---

452   1 Kings 18:40. NRS.

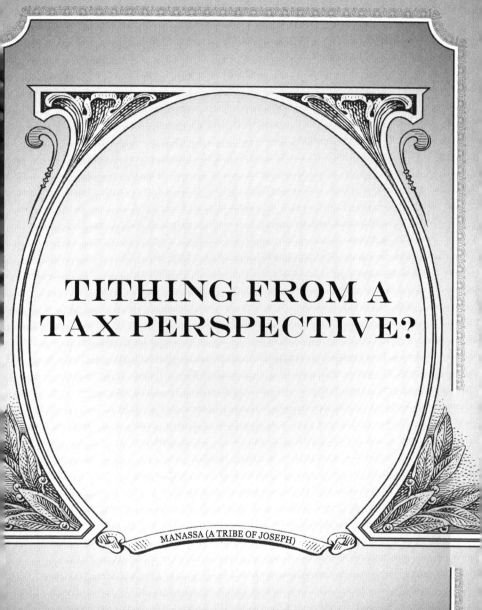

TITHING FROM A
TAX PERSPECTIVE?

MANASSA (A TRIBE OF JOSEPH)

CHAPTER EIGHT

Tithing, what the *%@8 does tithing to a Church have to do with taxes?

Tithing is:

1. A tenth part of one's annual income contributed voluntarily or due as a tax, especially for the support of the clergy or Church.
2. The institution or obligation of paying tithes.
3. A tenth part.
4. A very small part.[453]

*"Forget about the fourth definition, "**a very small part**," Is he talking about giving my hard earned money to the Church? Get your coat and get your hat. Let's start running and that's that." "Don't push me!"*

Before you run and shut down, *"help me, help you."*[454]   If you would allow, I would like to discuss tithing from a tax perspective. You see, from a tax perspective, tithing is your friend, your buddy, and your good old pal.

"Tithing From A Tax Perspective" discusses tithing from three perspectives: Biblical, Mathematical and Personal. It is my prayer that you will embrace the tithing concept and simultaneously increase your refund or lower your tax liability; not to mention get blessed in the process.

Biblically

God is essentially asking His people to tithe in order to support the Church.[455] Our tithes support Church operations, salaries, and other essential necessities. Here's the kicker. God not only ask us to tithe, but He says *"Test Me."* Test Me?[456] *Yes, Test Me!* In other words, *"I double*

---

453   The American Heritage® Dictionary of the English Language, Fourth Edition Copyright © 2006 by Houghton Mifflin Company. Published by Houghton Mifflin Company. All rights reserved. (As cited on "Dictionary.com") Origin: bef. 900; (n.) ME ti(ghe)the, OE teogotha TENTH; (v.) M.E. tithen, O.E. teogothian to take the tenth of, deriv. of the n.

454   *See* "Jerry McGuire." *Supra* cited at Footnote 426.

455   Malachi 3:10 NRS Bring the full tithe into the storehouse, so that there may be food in my house.

456   Malachi 3:10, NRS.

quadruple infinity dare you to tithe."

The premise is simple. If you tithe, then God will open the floodgates of heaven and pour out so many blessings there will not be enough room to hold them all.[457] In addition, He says, if you tithe, then He will hold the devourer from your finances[458] (Discussed further in "Personal" perspective).

The possibility of a flood gate of blessings is extremely appealing to me, especially in light of the fact that God is only asking for "a small part.[459]" *A small part? Dude, my current salary is seventy thousand dollars ($70,000) and God is asking for seven thousand dollars ($7,000). This ain't no small part!*

Actually, it's all a matter of perspective and what you believe. Many times when speaking at seminars, I present the follow scenario. I begin by holding an apple and asking who can create an apple. Many hands go up and individuals emphatically state how they can plant a seed, water it, nurture it and eventually a tree will grow bearing the fruit of an apple. *Good answer, but it's not the answer to the question.* I asked who can create an apple not who can grow an apple.

For only God can create an apple. No one on this green earth can make the sun shine, rain flow, or create the seed itself. Therefore, we begin with the precept that everything belongs to God and we are just stewards.

Then, I place ten (10) apples on a table and ask the audience to loudly count the number of apples. One, Two, Three, Four, Five, Six, Seven, Eight, Nine, Ten.

After counting to ten (10), I ask, *If everything belongs to God and we are just stewards, are you unwilling to give God just one (1) apple even*

---

457 *Id.*
458 Malachi 3:11, NRS.
459 *See* The American Heritage, *Supra* cited at Footnote 453.

though it all belongs to Him." Suddenly, there is a sense of deafening silence and revelation.

God is only asking for a tenth (1/10) of what He graciously bestows. Yet, we can't even give Him one (1) Granny Smith sour apple. I submit, the discomfort arises when we transfer the concept from fruits and seeds to actually tithing money, paper, cheese, or scrilla. Maybe, the challenge is we focus on what we're giving instead of what we will receive. For some reason, we hold on to money and idolize it as if it can save us from all calamities and bring true happiness.

From my experience, money can't buy you good health or happiness. Don't get me wrong; I too, am only human. *Money can't bring you happiness, but I sure would like to have enough to completely pay off my student loans and buy a moon pie for dessert.* I have also heard too many times, "More Money, More Problems." *Hell, I got problems already, so why not have them with money.*

The crux of this chapter is not in the giving or in the receiving, but rather in the fact that God dares us to "Test Him.[460]" That is, God double secret dares you to tithe and see if He won't keep his Word. Since God is not a man, He cannot lie.[461] This is the closest bet to a sure thing that anyone can possibly encounter. At a minimum, just like with prayer, it sure can't hurt.

Let's see. You tithe, God blesses you and you get a reduction in your taxes? Ding, ding, ding. Now, you're talking. *(Forget about that God and blessing stuff, how do I reduce my taxes?)*

Before we get to that point, my friend, I think that we should count our blessings. *Huh!* God could have asked for all of it. That's right, all. *"God wouldn't do that. Would He?"*

---

460 Malachi 3:10
461 Numbers 23:19 KJV

Dead As A Door Nail[462]

Once upon a time, there was a crippled man named "Joe" who had a professional job as a "beggar." Joe had it all figured out. Every day, the people would carry Joe to the Beautiful Gate at the entrance of the temple. While the people were enamored by the Beautiful Gate, Joe would hit them up for a piece of silver or gold and the people would more than likely comply. Oh, Joe had it good with an eighty-five percent (85%) success rate.

Peter and John were Apostle "Road Dogs"[463] and one day, they were headed to the temple for prayer. When Joe saw Peter and John, he thought to himself, here is an opportunity to get some "alms" (paper, dough, cheese, scrilla). *"Hey brother, can you spare a quarter so I can get something to eat?"*

Peter and John locked in on Joe and intently said *"Look at us."* Joe stared feverishly, anxiously anticipating a big haul, but he was in for the surprise and blessing of a lifetime.

As Joe was holding out his hand, expecting a nice piece of "scrilla," Peter said: *"I have no silver or gold, but what I have,[464] I give you; in the name of Jesus Christ of Nazareth, stand up and walk."* Then Peter took Joe by the right hand and raised him up; and immediately his feet and ankles were made strong. *Jesus, you truly are the Son of God!*

The people knew Joe well and they looked in wonder and amazement, and began praising God. In spite of their bewilderment, Peter was appalled. He reminded them of how Pilate wanted to release Jesus and how they crucified him instead of releasing a convicted murderer.

Of course, hindsight is twenty-twenty. Plus, Peter didn't realize everything had to play itself out in order for Christianity to become the religion that it is.

---

462 This story is based on Acts Chapters 3-5.
463 "Traveling Partner"
464 Comma intentionally inserted for understanding.

Meanwhile, Annas, Caiaphas, John and Alexander (all members of the High Priest Council), were chilling in the roman baths, feasting on vino, grapes and other delicacies, when, all of a sudden, they got word of another Jesus sighting. *"I thought we got rid of that Jesus guy and his followers the other day. Arrest them and bring them before the High Council."*

Peter and John were immediately arrested and the people followed in expectation. The high priest's question was straight and to the point. *"By what power or by what name did you do this?"*

Peter was filled with the Holy Ghost and said:

> Rulers of the people and elders, if we are questioned today because of a good deed done to someone who was sick and are asked how this man has been healed, let it be known to all of you, and to all the people of Israel, that this man is standing before you in good health by the name of Jesus Christ of Nazareth, whom you crucified, whom God raised from the dead. This Jesus is "the stone that was rejected by you, the builders; it has become the cornerstone. There is salvation in no one else, for there is no other name under heaven given among mortals by which we must be saved.

Wow, is this the same Peter that Christ foretold would deny him before the cock crows three times?[465] The high priests were amazed and knew they were in a precarious situation. They recognized Peter and John as part of the Jesus Crew.

The high priest looked at Peter and John with a daunting stare. He knew they were "uneducated and ordinary" men; yet they spoke with boldness, clarity and fulfillment. Then, they looked at Joe who was dancing like James Brown doing the camel walk. With all of this going on, the proverbial cat had every one of the high priests' tongues.

So, they convened privately and said:

---

465   John Chap.13:36-38 (NRS).

What will we do with them? For it is obvious to all who live in Jerusalem that a notable sign has been done through them; we cannot deny it. But to keep it from spreading further among the people, let us warn them to speak no more to anyone in this name.

But Peter and John weren't backing down. They replied:

Whether it is right in God's sight to listen to you rather than to God, you must judge; for we cannot keep from speaking about what we have seen and heard.

There was no way to punish them. So the high priest were given a stern warning and let go.

Peter and John turned and walked away from the high priest completely unscathed and full of confidence. *"Don't you know that my name is Peter and I was one of the original twelve (12). You better recognize Jesus' Boys when you see them. Peace Out!"*

After they were released, Peter and John went back and told what had happened and when the people heard it, they raised their voices as high as the highest trumpets and they prayed harder than a politician on Election Day. Then, the building shook; they were filled with the Holy Spirit.

Everyone was feeling so good that everything was on one accord. There was one heart, one love, one soul, and one wallet. That's right! Everyone took all of their worldly possessions, sold them, and laid all of the money at the apostles' feet. The apostles then distributed the proceeds according to each person's needs. Miraculously, there was not a needy person in the camp. Let me repeat that *"there was not a needy person in the camp."*

Levite was from Cyprus, but, in the Jesus Crew, he was known as "Barnabas." Levite sold his field for a nice price and boldly laid it at the apostles' feet.

You can bet your bottom dollar; however, that there is always a knuckle head in the group. Well, this time, the tense is plural. There was not one, but two knuckle heads and, to make it worse, they were husband and wife.

Annanias and Sapphira knew the two fundamental rules of real estate:

1) Location, Location, Location; and
2) Buy Low and Sell High.

So, they purchased some property in Jerusalem during the pinnacle of the Jesus frenzy and held on to it until after He was crucified. Naturally, the property sky rocketed and they sold the property without a hitch. Regrettably, they were not convinced by this new "community, all for one and one for all thing."

That evening, Ananias approached his wife:

> "Honey, don't get me wrong, I'm with this Jesus thing and everything, but we're giving up a lot of money. Yeah, Barnabas gave a lot of money, but for the most part, no one is making the same sacrifice that we're making and it's not fair."

Sapphira replied:

> Honey, I didn't want to say anything, because I knew that you wanted to be a part of the Jesus Crew, but I do agree. Why don't you give ninety percent and a small part? Anyway, our ninety percent is more than half of the whole community pot anyway.

It was a plan. Ananias kept a small part of the proceeds and laid the rest of the proceeds at the apostles' feet. As soon as the money hit the ground, Peter asked him:

> "Why has Satan filled your heart to lie to the Holy Spirit and to keep back part of the proceeds of the land? While it remained unsold, did it not remain your own? And after it was sold, were

not the proceeds at your disposal? How is it that you have contrived this deed in your heart? You did not lie to us but to God!

When Ananias heard these words, he fell down "Dead As A Door Nail," and the people were paralyzed with fear. The young men wrapped his body, carried him away, and buried him.

Meanwhile, Sapphira was in the market, eyeing a pair of Gucci sandals, when she realized she was late for her temple appointment. Sapphira was happy as a lark, skipping in her new Gucci sandals that she purchased with her portion of the money withheld.

Three hours after Ananias' death, Sapphira arrived at the temple and didn't have a clue about her husband's supernatural encounter.

Peter asked her: "Sapphira, did you sell your property for three hundred thousand drekels ($300,000)?

Sapphira replied: *"Yes, that was the price."*

Peter then said: *"How is it that you have agreed together to put the Spirit of the Lord to the test. Look at the feet of the young men who are standing at the door. These are the feet that buried your husband and these are the same feet that will bury you.*

Upon hearing these words, Sapphira fell down "Dead As A Door Nail" and was buried beside her husband. Needless to say, great fear seized the whole Church and the news spread like wild fire.

Meanwhile, Matthew was out of town, and didn't know about the Jesus miracle with Joe the Beggar. When Matthew approached the town, he noticed the heightened spirit level and heard some people talking about some kinda *"one accord"* thing. Matthew saw his neighbor and asked, "What in the world is happening?"

Joe the Beggar from the Beautiful Gate got healed and was seen moon walking down Selah Boulevard. The Jesus Apostle Boys were hemmed up[466] by the High Council; stood their ground; and were eventually released. Because of all of the wonderful miracles, the people sold all of their possessions and were on one accord; while, Ananias and Sapphire withheld a *small part* of their money and fell out, "Dead As A Doornail."

Matthew knew Joe the beggar and, after seeing the people, he sold all of his possessions; gave God all of the glory; and began celebrating His goodness.

The End

Ananias and Sapphire withheld a *small portion*, and were killed dead as a door nail. Yet, here we are complaining about giving a small portion. Matters not that all of it belongs to God and we are just stewards. But we get caught up in: *"What's the preacher gonna do with my money?"* and *"Did you hear that the minister purchased a brand new Cadillac for himself and a Bentley for his wife?"*

God didn't ask you to test the Preacher, Rabbi, Minister, or Buddha. God said, *"Test Me!"*[467]

Surely, if God is omnipotent, and He is, then He is more than capable of addressing any misappropriation of His tithes and offerings. So, why should we worry over such insignificant matters to which we have no control?

Exactly! We shouldn't. Just *"Test Him."* I double quadruple infinity dare you. Just *"Test Him."*

Mathematically

One of the purest forms of science is mathematics. Even though the numbers may change, the rules remain the same; that is, addition is

---

466 "arrested"
467 *See* Malachi 3:10 NRS.

addition and subtraction is subtraction. Mathematics is the world's universal language. One (1) is equal to one (1) whether it's in English, Chinese, Swahili, or French. With this in mind, let's explore tithing from a mathematical perspective.

Once upon a time there were two taxpayers, Ms. Jones and Mr. White. They each owned a home in a nice suburban neighborhood. Sister Jones attended the 45th Avenue Church of Hope & Prosperity and Mr. White was an atheist. For simplicity, let's say that both Taxpayers had an adjusted gross income of fifty thousand dollars ($50,000).

Form 1040

Adjusted Gross Income[468]	
Ms. Jones	50,000
Ms. White	50,000

After calculating your AGI, you may deduct the larger of a standard deduction or itemized deductions. Most of the time, taxpayers can only take advantage of itemized deductions when they own a home and deduct the mortgage payments. Otherwise, the itemized deductions total does not exceed the standard deduction.

Wait a minute. That's not fair. I rent my home and pay an amount very similar to a mortgage. Moreover, both abodes are used for shelter purposes. Why can't I deduct my rent? Sorry my friend, that's the way the Original Gangsta *rolls.*[469]

The list of itemized deductions is comprised of a number of different transactions including:

- Medical expenses paid[470]

---

468   Remember your adjusted gross income is nothing more than your gross income (dough, paper, scrilla) minus any statutory adjustments such as moving expenses, one-half of your self employment taxes, etc.

469   "operates"

470   Note: Medical Expenses can be claimed as an itemized deduction if the cost was incurred versus reimbursed by an insurance company. In addition, it is also subject to a 7.5% limitation; hence, it is very difficult to satisfy.

- State taxes withheld
- Real estate taxes paid
- Mortgage Interest Paid
- Casualty Loses and
- Charitable Contributions
  - Cash
  - Noncash

Sister Jones and Mr. White had the following Schedule A, Itemized Deductions:

	Ms. Jones	Mr. White
Mortgage Interest	8,000	8,000
State Taxes Withheld	754	754
Real Estate Taxes	1,200	1,200
Charitable Cash Contributions	5,000	-0-
Total:	**14,954**	**9,954**

After this, the math is fairly simple:

	Ms. Jones	Mr. White
Adjusted Gross Income	50,000	50,000
<Itemized Deductions>	-14,954	-9,954
Exemptions	-3,500	-3,500
Taxable Income	31,546	36,546
Taxes Owed	4,328	5,475

By tithing, Sister Jones paid one thousand, one hundred and forty-seven dollars ($1,147.00) **less** in taxes. This tax savings is only the small picture. The big picture is Sister Jones not only reduced her tax liability, but she also received God's blessings. Consequently, Sister Jones was killing two proverbial birds with one tithing stone.

Most importantly, you have a fundamental choice - either you're going to give your money to God or you're going to give it to the Internal Revenue

Service. That is, if you don't tithe, the increase in tax is going directly to the Original Gangsta.

Instead of making a charitable contribution and doing some good, Mr. White's contribution was zero and the Original Gangsta sucked his money up like a high power commercial vacuum cleaner. And what did Mr. White get in return? Nothing, nada, zilch!

The beautiful thing about the whole situation is the Original Gangsta does not require you to make your charitable donation to a Church. The Original Gangsta only requires you to donate to an Internal Revenue Code §501(c)(3) tax-exempt organization. Since the creation of faith-based initiatives instituted by President Bush, more nonprofits exist today than we can shake a money stick at.

The fact that Mr. White is an atheist is irrelevant for tax purposes. Mr. White can still give to a worthy cause like his former university, the Salvation Army, Goodwill, Cancer Fund, etc. As long as he obtains a receipt, *it's all good.*[471]

However, Mr. White will not receive the full benefit of his contribution. If he were to tithe, then he would receive the tax benefit and God's blessings, too. Why not get two for the price of one?

<u>Personally</u>

I believe in tithing a tenth of your time, talent and money. I also believe tithing is a personal thang,[472] between you and God. I started tithing ten percent (10%) of my net income during the 70's. It was not until years later that I grew to tithe ten percent (10%) of my *gross*.

I always like to keep it real and straight across the board. **If you begin tithing, then you must continue.** Otherwise, you will see how much God is keeping the devourer off your finances.[473]

471　"everything is honky dory."
472　"thing"
473　Malachi 3:11 New Revised Standard (NRS)

I distinctly remember living in Madison, New Jersey and being faced with a challenging question: Do I tithe or do I pay the electric bill? Little did I know this was a test, and unfortunately, I failed. I paid the electric bill. The very next day, all of a sudden, creditors came from no where, emphatically stating that there were balances that were owed on accounts that I never knew existed.

Lesson learned. From now on, if I'm faced with that choice, then I make sure and tithe.

When I moved to Atlanta and started TaxConcepts, I later learned, if you really want to get blessed, then one should not only tithe but also provide additional offerings to assist in God's ministry. As a result, God presented me with a most unique charitable contribution/tithing/offering opportunity.

During this time, I was not making a lot of money and, if I received one hundred and fifty dollars ($150.00) for a consultation, then I was as happy as a kid in a candy store. God knew of my commitment to tithe a tenth of my gross; however, He asked me if I trusted Him enough to tithe and match my gifts by the amount of the tithe and add one more dollar.

So, upon receiving the one hundred and fifty dollars ($150.00) from a consultation, I would

Tithe Ten Percent (10%)	$15.00
Gift Match Tithe	$15.00
Add At Least One Dollar More	$ 1.00
Total Charitable Contribution	$31.00

As I look back, I know it was nothing but the grace of God that carried me through the first year. I didn't make the change of nickel, yet I never missed a meal and actually gained five pounds in the process.

The challenge was not tithing the one hundred and fifty dollars ($150.00) consultation fee, but rather the retainer fee for three thousand dollars ($3,000.00):

Tithe Ten Percent (10%)	$300.00
Gift Match Tithe	$300.00
Add At Least One Dollar More	$ 1.00
Total Charitable Contribution	$601.00

Although those extra three hundred and one pieces of gold may not sound like much to you, trust me, when you're starting your own business from scratch, three hundred and one dollars ($301.00) is a mint. For an entire year, I kept my word and I know that's why God blessed me so much.

To this very day, I continue to tithe ten percent of my gross. As a matter of fact, God wants His share *up front*[474] and in this day of modern electronics, I make sure that it happens. When I receive a consultation fee, the check is deposited into our bank account. I check the internet to make sure the check has cleared and, once it has, I tithe visa-a-vie an electronic transfer. This way: 1) God receives His before I get mine; 2) I get the charitable deduction not to mention adequate records (See Prepare for War During A Time of Peace); and 3) I get blessed in the process.

In spite of this fantastic news, there are some who believe tithing is not scriptural. Their arguments are based on:

- Tithing was a concept in the Old Testament and we live under the New Testament[475]
- Only Levite Priest were allowed to collect tithes and Levite Priest are no longer a priesthood of the Church[476]
- Only agricultural products (fruits, vegetables, seeds) were tithable[477]
- Money was never a tithable commodity[478]

---

474 "first"
475 "Tithing Is Unscriptural Under The New Covenant" [A Scriptural Exposition On The Fraudulent Fleecing Of The Flock] http://bible-truths.com.
476 *Id.*
477 *Id.*
478 *Id.*

Moreover, what happens if the Preacher buys his wife two fur coats and diamond earrings with my hard earned money? Again, I submit that your focus is misplaced. If God tells you to do it and you will be rewarded, then "do it." God said, "*Test Me*[479]."

Take heed and hold God to His Word. Try Him, He'll never fail you. I invite you to take advantage man, take advantage.

Oh, by the way, the gentleman who professed that tithing is not scriptural is now suffering from terminal prostate cancer which metastasized a year ago throughout his skull, spine, arms, legs, shoulders, hips and pelvis.[480] *Coincidence?* You decide.

---

479 Malachi 3:10, New Revised Standard
480 Malachi 3:9

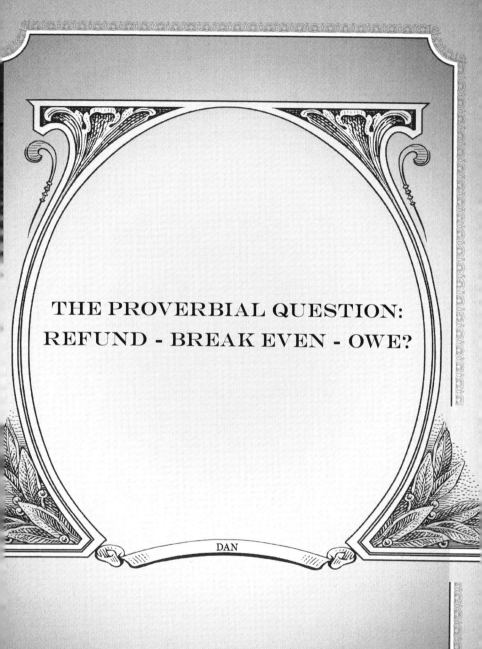

THE PROVERBIAL QUESTION:
REFUND - BREAK EVEN - OWE?

DAN

CHAPTER NINE

REFUND

Like everyone else, I remember my very first job. I was fourteen (14) and employed as bag boy at Foodtown in Savannah, Georgia. Three weekdays and every Saturday I would carefully, yet quickly and efficiently load each customer's paper bag of groceries.

By the time the customer paid the cashier, the groceries were bagged, bread and eggs always separately, and I was standing by the cart ready to push it to the car, load it up, and receive that oh-so-precious tip.

In addition to the tips, I also received a salary. I started my job at the end of the payroll period, so I didn't accumulate many hours. But when that Saturday pay day came around, I was happy nonetheless. My very first check! Are you kidding me? I'm the Man. *Wait a minute, what is this Federal, State and F.I.C.A. thing?*

One of my ace dogs who taught me how to "*hustle*" [481] also broke this tax thing down. [482] I didn't quite understand it, but he made it pretty clear that there was no getting around it. Wow. Bummer. *Anyway, where do I go to cash my check?*

The next week I worked twice as many hours and I was even more excited, because I had it all figured out. My base salary is X and I worked 40 hours, so, my income was 40 times X or 40X.

Now that I knew about this tax thing, I couldn't leave it out. Last week, I worked 20 hours and the total taxes withheld were $100. Simple mathematical deduction; my salary calculation was:

Paycheck = (40 times X) - $100 (taxes)

When I got my check, I was floored. *Hey, what happen to the rest of my money? You guys withheld too much taxes and I need it now!*

---

481 Work extremely hard until you reach your desired goal. Note: A true hustler's goals constantly change; hence, he (or she) is always "hustling."
482 Explained it to me.

I was furious, and then my ace dog "pulled my coat tail."[483] *Oh, I forgot to tell you, the more you make, the more they take.*

This was my first cognizant introduction to the "Original Gangsta." The more you make, the more they take. What kind of madness is this?

This tax thing threw my focus into a complete frenzy. *You messin' wit*[484] *my money!* I started dropping cans of beans on top of loaves of bread and those poor eggs didn't have a chance. One day, I placed the eggs at the bottom of the bag; then dropped a ripe cantaloupe right on top of it. I had to start focusing or there would be no tax thing, because there would be no job thing.

I continued working and going to school. I wish that I could say I saved and invested my earnings, but that would be a lie. I bought clothes and roller skates so I could impress the girls. *Come on, I was 14 years old. What else was I suppose to do?*

Well, spring rolled around and happy days were here again. I discovered you could file a piece of paper and get all of the money back you gave the government during the year. *Yeah Man! This tax thing ain't so bad; I got a refund and all of my money back.*

Like most Americans, every April 15th, I filed a government-generated form and received my money back in the form of a refund. I, and many others, always believed the Government was giving us some sort of gift in the way of a refund. Actually, we are just belatedly receiving the same money withheld from our paycheck each week. Much later, I discovered that classic tax studies dictate it's better to "break even or owe small amounts."

When you're fourteen and making three hundred dollars ($300.00) a week, you get all of your money back. But when you're in your 30's, married with kids, and own two cars and pay a mortgage, the story is just a little different.

---

483   To enlighten; provide wisdom or knowledge; show one the way.
484   "messing with"

First, we must determine the amount of tax that is owed. If more money was withheld than the amount of tax, then, and only then, will you receive a refund. However, if the tax is more than the amount withheld, then, *Sorry Charlie*,[485] no refund; you owe the government.

The worst part is as we get older, we realize we're not making any interest off the money withheld by the Original Gangsta. That's why it's said when you receive a refund, you're giving the Government an interest-free loan. You give the Government your money and it gives it back to you, interest free. What a wonderful concept. *Capitalism at it's best*.[486]

I remember speaking at a forum and after presenting the proverbial question (Refund, Breakeven, Owe), one gentleman boldly proclaimed: "Everybody knows it's better to receive a refund. Last year, I received $15,000."

Then, I asked him the following:

- How much interest did the Government give you for the use of your $15,000.00?
- What investments could you have taken advantage of during the year with $15,000 smakaroos?[487]
- How much scrilla[488] could you make from investing $15,000.00 (even in the most conservative investment vehicle like a bond)?

After lifting the veil from his eyes, I could see his brain moving a thousand miles a second. *But how do I break even, because I definitely don't want to pay the government?*

---

485 *See Star Wars, Supra* cited at Footnote 392.
486 Capitalism at it's best! Every time I see that phrase, I can't help but envision Don King waving an American Flag and saying "Only in America."
487 Smakaroos is a synonym of "dollars".
488 "Money"

BREAKEVEN

Usually, the human resource department presents a Form W4, among other numerous forms, when we first start our job. The Form W4 discusses exemptions, dependents, numbers, withholding and a whole bunch of other stuff we have no clue about. We pick a number; sign the form; go to work; and wait for our first check.

Like Russian roulette, we wait till the end of the year; hand our receipts and other financials to the tax preparer; and wait for the surprise. *Did we get a refund or do we owe?*

Note: To get a good idea about the amount to withhold, check out the withholding calculator at the IRS' website. Go to www.irs.gov and click on "Withholding Calculator" under "Online Services."

Breaking even requires you to constantly evaluate your taxable transactions during the year. If you get it just right, you won't owe the government and the government won't owe you. In order to break even, your withholding must match your actual tax liability. If you don't withhold enough then you owe taxes and you may incur interest and, possibly, penalties. If you withhold too much, you give the government an interest-free loan and lose out on the present use of your money while it's withheld.

The key to breaking even is simply a matter of paying attention. If there are personal, financial or legal changes in your life or the law, then your tax liability also will more than likely change. For example:

Personal Changes:

- Marriage
- Divorce
- Birth/Adoption of a Child
- New Home Purchase
- Retirement
- Chapter 11 Bankruptcy

Financial Changes:

- Interest Income
- Dividends
- Capital Gains
- Self-Employment Income
- IRS Distributions

Legal Changes:

- This one requires the most work. You gotta go to the www.irs.gov; click on "Forms and Publications;" thereafter, click on "What's Hot in Forms and Publications." Note: Each lifestyle factor is evaluated each year in preparation for the upcoming tax filing.

After evaluating each of these potential changes, it you determine you're not withholding enough, then you submit a new Form W4 to your human resource department; reduce your allowances; and/or provide an additional amount to be withheld each pay period. If it is determined you are withholding too much, then your new Form W4 will reflect an increase in your allowances. *It's just that simple!*

Well, actually it's not that simple! You must first translate your transactions into numbers. Worksheets are computed and reviewed; and Government forms calculated; signed, copied and filed. *Gee whiz. Thanks Mr. Smarty Pants. You're responsible for bringing us to this tax enigma and all you have for us is more work? Thanks a lot, but no thanks.* There is an alternative. *Thank You Jesus!*

Speak with your tax professional; notify him/her or any changes; and let him/her do all of the work. Some preparers may charge an additional fee; some may be incapable of handling the intellectual exercise; and others may even be like the gas station tax preparer and tell you the Government stopped offering this option three years ago so changing your allowances will arouse suspicion.

Trust your feelings Luke.[489] First, hire an ethical tax professional who knows the law or is at least willing to read it on the website. *Good luck on that one!*

Second, in conjunction with an able tax professional, you must simultaneously observe your personal and financial lifestyle changes. Observation, creative thinking, and communication will enhance the chance of breaking even tremendously.

If you don't quite break even, then you can probably come pretty close. You may even get a small refund or owe a small amount. *Then again, is it really that bad if we owe the Government?*

OWE

Well, if I follow your suggestion, then maybe I'll owe the government a small amount like five hundred dollars ($500). That's a good thing, right?

It's a great thing. Remember our old mantra, "Render Unto Caesar, That Which Is Caesar's, But Nothing More?" If you owe the Government five hundred dollars ($500) and pay it off by April 15th, not only have you not left any money on the table, you've taken the table, lamplight, and books with you as you're walking out the door.[490]

If you owe the Government a small tax liability and you timely file your return, plus submit the proper payment by April 15th or before; then you have essentially obtained an interest-free loan from the Government.

That's right! You took out a small no interest loan from the government. You file the forms; pay the tax liability; and have a nice day. *BTW*[491], *thanks for the loan.* Hopefully either you've earned some interest or used the loan for investment in a business.

---

489   *See* Star Wars, *Supra* at Footnote 392.
490   You maximized the transaction to its most infinite optimum results.
491   "By The Way"

Before you get too excited, *let me introduce you to my little friend, Mr. Estimated Tax Man, and he be real bad.*[492] That is, he's a very mean man.

Mr. Estimated Tax Man normally leans[493] on the portion of income that is not subject to withholding:

- Self-employment income
- Interest
- Dividends
- Alimony
- Rent
- Gains from the sale of assets
- Prizes and awards.

If you don't withhold enough taxes, Mr. Estimated Tax Man will probably give you a little visit carrying a baseball bat over his shoulder, Original Gangsta style.

Mr. Estimated Tax Man preys on income tax; self-employment tax; as well as other taxes and amounts reported on your tax return. Before you complain about the tax, we're just getting started.

Mr. Estimated Tax Man will penalize you if you don't withhold enough and/or you don't pay enough by the due date of each payment period. Mr. Estimated Tax Man can use his penalty baseball bat even if you are due a refund when you file your return. So how do you identify that magical bench mark of penalty or no penalty?

Mr. Estimated Tax Man is a complex formula involving yearly analysis, withholding and credit subtractions, and percentage calculations. Truthfully, as with most complex formulas, I try to apply the old adage: Why work harder, when you can work smarter? Put the information in a software program and press "enter." Consult your tax professional and request assistance with Mr. Estimated Tax Man.

---

492 "is very bad"
493 "is applicable to"

Provided that you've got Mr. Estimated Tax Man somewhat in *check*[494], then owing the Original Gangsta isn't such a bad *"thang."*[495] The real question is, "Did you get more than you gave?" If the rate of return on your investment is less than the interest on your taxes, then owing the Original Gangsta doesn't appear to be a good idea. If your investment's rate of return is higher than the Original Gangsta's, then, maybe it's worth considering.

Yet, in spite of all of its benefits, "owing" the Government is not the answer to the proverbial question (refund-breakeven-owe).

PROVERBIAL ANSWER

Unfortunately, neither receiving a happy dance, feel-good refund; nor breaking even; or even owing the Government is the proverbial answer. The answer to the Proverbial Question is: *"It depends"*

We're all different people, with different personalities and preferences. Thus, the Proverbial Answer "depends" on *"who you are"* and *"what cha like."*[496]

Some people like to receive a fat juicy refund and that's okay. *"If you like getting a refund, get a refund."* Just make sure you're smart with it. Spend some of it on yourself and family; but also invest the majority into a vehicle that will generate income.

If you like breaking even, "break even." Perform the mathematical gymnastics and consult your able tax professional. At the end of the year, you don't owe the Original Gangsta and the Original Gangsta doesn't owe you.

If you like receiving an interest - free loan or paying Mr. Estimated Tax Man on the loan, then "it's all gud."[497] As long as you used the funds

---

494 "analyzed the potential negative ramifications and planned appropriately"
495 "thing"
496 "what you like."
497 "Everything is alright."

to construct a new building, capital for an entrepreneurial venture, or investment in a business partnership, then, it's not so bad.

For years, I loved getting "refunds," because I believed I was getting something for nothing. After becoming a tax attorney, I grew to embrace "breaking even." With the genesis of my business, I discovered "*it depends*" is a true reality. It was not until I began speaking in seminars, that I developed my current philosophy.

On one occasion, I asked the proverbial question. Upon hearing numerous answers, I was about to provide my proverbial answer of "*it depends*" when it hit me. You really want to "*owe*" the Original Gangsta. More specifically, you want to owe the Original Gangsta hundreds of millions of dollars in taxes.

Why? If you owe hundreds of millions of dollars in taxes, you gotta to be making billions! *Do you wanna be a billionaire?*

I'm sure that being a billionaire has it challenges, but at least, if you don't like the experience, you can always give the money away and go back to working nine to five. "*Yeah, right.*"

Ultimately, the proverbial answer may morph with different stages in your life. If you aspire to owe the Government hundreds of millions in dollars," then, don't stop there. Elevate your mind to owe, billions, trillions, or even gazillions. If you're at the point where you want a big fat juicy refund, then, that's okay too. Again, in the end, the proverbial answer to the proverbial question is, "*It depends.*"

A CONVERSATION WITH MRS. SERVICE, EMPLOYEE ID #77-77777

ASHER

CHAPTER TEN

Like I said, I'm not the sharpest knife in the drawer and I never did really get it when we were taught "taxes are socially driven." Now, I get it.

Once upon a time, in the early days of business, I was so small I was the tax attorney, trash man, administrative assistant, computer consultant, and security guard. One day, I received a frantic call from a new client.

She received a certified letter from the Original Gangsta and didn't know what to do. I informed her to fax the letter immediately and we would take care of it. Even though it was just me, I always believed in maintaining a corporate "us" perspective.

The letter stated there was an error in the return we prepared. More specifically, the letter stated that we either "calculated the self employment taxes incorrectly or placed them on the wrong line."

Nobody's perfect and everybody makes mistakes; however, as an attorney, I gotta[498] problem. Attorneys are trained to specifically dissect even the most minute word such as "or." Thus, which one is it? Did we *calculate it incorrectly; did we put it in the wrong place; or are you just trying to hustle me? Hhhhhhmmmmm!*

Immediately, I reviewed the return and called the Original Gangsta to resolve the matter. When I worked for the Original Gangsta and taxpayers would call, I never said *"please"* or *"thank you."* Either you provided me with the appropriate information or speak to my manager who would tell you the same thing. Now that I am on the opposite side of the phone, it's a completely different story.

"My name is Mrs. Service and my identification number is 77-77777. How may I help you?"

Good morning Mrs. Service. How are you today?

---

498 "have"

Manners and kindness goes a long way. As a Good Ole Southern Boy, I was taught you can get more from flies with honey than you can with vinegar. To put it in Original Gangsta terms, respect will get you in the door. On this day, Mrs. Service was having none of that.

How may I help you? (Spoken in a curt tone)

Mrs. Service, we represent Client and we received Letter 941. We would appreciate it greatly if you could provide some clarity.

Like the letter states, either you calculated the taxes incorrectly or you placed them in the wrong place.

I wanted to say: Look lady, I've taken too many test, at too many schools, including the Georgia Bar, to not comprehend a statement consisting of no more than four (4) syllables per word. In other words, "Look lady, I know how to read." Emphasis on *"wanted to say."*

Yes I know, but could you please assist us in understanding the content of the letter.

(Heavy and unprofessional sigh) Okay, what numbers do you have on page one, line 18.

I politely read the numbers from the return.

Well your self-employment taxes should have been $7,532.16.

Mrs. Service, we calculated the self-employment taxes and our total was "$7,532.16." The same number as your calculations.

Well, like the letter stated, you didn't put it in the right place.

I didn't respond by stating "we put the corresponding number on line 24." Why? You always give your enemy enough rope to hang themselves.

Mrs. Service, where should we have reported the self-employment calculations?

You should have put the self-employment calculations on line 24.

Mrs. Service, our return reflects a total of $7,532.16 on line 24.

There was a deafening silence over the phone for an uncomfortable amount of time.

Well, you have to write us a letter and tell us that we were wrong.

Mrs. Service, let me make sure I understand you correctly, we calculated the taxes correctly; put them on the correct line, and now we have to write you a letter, telling you that the mistake was yours?

That's right.

What's the address?

True Story!

THE REAL DEAL

"Pay attention to the man behind the curtain." Here's the real deal. In Washington, DC, at 1111 Constitution Avenue, NW on top of the IRS Headquarters building amidst the Roman Columns are the renowned words by Oliver Wendell Holmes: "Taxes Are What We Pay For A Civilized Society."

The "civilized society" during this period is smack dab[499] in the middle of the Iraq war. Coincidently, during this exact same time

---

499 "right in the middle"

period, surprisingly, there was an increase in audits.[500] Ask yourself this, how many taxpayers have received similar computer-generated letters and immediately paid the tax because of fear, ignorance, and/or intimidation? *Again I say, things that make you go Hhhhmmmmm!*

Instead of raising taxes for war, the Service decided to take them. These actions ring with the faint familiar sound and smell of the Original Gangsta. As I reiterated, "Pay Attention To The Man Behind The Curtain."

"Behind the Curtain," America was fighting the evil villain Sadam Hussein and Original Gangsta is responsible for getting the paper *hook, crook, or took!*[501] But I'm confused as to why we were fighting. First, you tell me our intelligence confirmed that Saddam Hussein had weapons of mass destruction. In midstream, you change your story to "Iraq Freedom." Our job is to free the people from Sadam's reign of terror. Then what do you know: *"Surprise, Surprise, Surprise,"*[502] we can't find any weapons of mass destruction.

Meanwhile, Bin Laden was on the run until President Obama captured him. As taxpayers, we need to always keep abreast of world and national events, because the politics of today will dictate the taxes of tomorrow.[503]

Currently, we're coming out of a recession. Gas prices are astronomical and the real estate market has gone so far South it has begun to use words like *"yall, eat cheese grits for breakfast, and drink sweet tea for lunch."*

We have the first African-American President who inherited the pillage of President Bush's carnage. Mr. Bush and Mr. Cheney made enough money in their eight year administration that their, great, great, great .

---

500   TIGTA, Final Audit Report-Trends In Compliance Activities Through Fiscal Year 2003, Reference Number: 2004-30-083) 4/23/2004.

501   "obtaining the money by any means necessary"

502   Gomer Pyle is a gentle, good-hearted, rural auto mechanic character played by Jim Nabors on the TV sitcom The Andy Griffith Show. He was often known for exclaiming "Surprise, Surprise, Surprise." Citing Wikipedia, the free encyclopedia (Gomer Pyle wikipedia)(http://en.wikipedia.org/wiki/Gomer_Pyle) (Retrieved April 30, 2012).

503   Lauren Z. Medlock Smith, Esq.

. . great, grand children's grand children will never have to worry about money again.

These times have been proclaimed the worst since the depression. Thus, in light of these challenging times, the Original Gangster showed that it has a heart the size of a small red dot on the top of an ant's antenna.

The Original Gangsta is more amenable than usual to establishing installment agreements (provided that you can prove that no one wants to buy your first born . . . *naw, just kidding*). As long as you work with them and stick to your deadlines, they will work with you. But if you ignore them and breach your payment arrangement, then it's back to "OG" business as usual.

Why? Because the Original Gangsta gotta[504] get that paper to rejuvenate our economy in order to finance other wars; opps, I'm sorry . . . "maintain peace."

Socially driven whatever, yah, yah, yah! That's not applicable to me. I don't need an installment agreement, because I didn't owe the IRS taxes last year. As a matter of fact, I got a fat[505] refund last year and I heard a fellow at a party say "taxes are unconstitutional anyway."

My dear friend, please remember, "pay attention to the man behind the curtain." The story ain't finished yet.   Ever wonder what happened to all of those accountants that were fired during the recession? Well, they went to work for the Original Gangsta as "Technical Reviewers" a.k.a. "Scouts." The Scouts' primary objective is to review tax returns and analyze them for deficiencies, inaccuracies, and inconsistencies.

Query: *If you just got fired from your last job and in the midst of a recession, the Original Gangsta hired you to find tax return errors . . . how many errors do you think you would find?*

Query: *If you were a Scout . . . how many errors do you think you could*

---

504 "has"
505 Huge, gigantic, enormous.

find if you were trained by the supreme tax authority in these United States and most taxpayers avoid taxes like the black plague's ugly cousin?

Query: *How many people have received, and will receive, letters from Mrs. Service and pay the tax out of fear and/or lack of knowledge?*

And guess what? Audits are still on the rise! Chris Wagner, IRS SB/SE Commissioner, recently stated:

Exams will rise for two reasons. We are trying to be successful in what we do. We want to work more cases than we did the year before.[506]

Wow! That's deep! The Original Gangsta is not increasing exams because of inaccuracies, policy abuses, or a change in our social climate. Basically, its' raising taxes because:

1. That's what the Original Gangsta does, fool. Recognize.[507]
2. Our paper stack is short and we gotta knock some heads around to get it back up.[508]

I defy you to tell me that the IRS is not gangsta. *Don't hate the player, learn from the game.* It's brilliant.

The Original Gangsta's scout program generates revenue to replenish the stimulus money given by President Bush and President Obama's administrations. *Mommy, there go that Man behind the curtain again!*

Taking taxes and hiring scouts are ingeniously creative vehicles to raise money; however, they are merely derivatives from our good friend William Pitt. You remember him from "The Big Hustle." The guy who implemented the income tax and the media sell to fund the war.

---

506   CPA Magazine, Volume 8, No. 5 (October 2009), IRS Exams Will rise IRS SB/SE Commissioner, Chris Wagner, Steel Rose, CPA. Page 16.
507   That's how we operate.
508   Our bank account is dwindling and it's necessary to generate additional funds.

I ain't mad![509] Thinking of new vehicles to collect taxes is what Original Gangstas do!

While that's all well and good, *"Conversations With Mrs. Service ID #77-7777"* cost our clients enormous legal representation fees, often defending that which was initially presented correctly.

In spite of these inequitable methodologies, we are expected to "Render Unto Caesar." *You dog gone skippy.* You better render or Caesar will seize. *It ain't fair! It just ain't fair!*

Is it that it ain't fair or that we haven't figured out how to play the game? We've got to get our minds' right. When our minds' are right, we can successfully lessen our tax liability and defend our innocence against the Original Gangsta.

When our minds are right, we can establish a coalition to defend citizens that have been unjustly violated by the Original Gangsta. When our minds are right, we can collectively unite to create a tax system designed to satisfy our fiscal responsibilities, while simultaneously not making taxpayers feel like they are being accosted. When our minds are right, we realize and understand how taxes are socially driven.

Don't be afraid to send your Congressperson a letter, demanding accountability and retribution. In the post script of our letter, you can also let him or her know, if we don't get what we want, then we're going public with suggestive pictures on the Jerry Springer Show[510] (*It's a joke, ha, ha . . . unless there really are some pictures*).

Yes, my friend, taxes are socially driven and it begins with YOU! Still think that taxes aren't socially driven?

---

509 "I am not upset or envious."
510 Jerry Springer Show is a syndicated television tabloid talk show distributed by NBC Universal Television Distribution. *See* http//en.wikipeida.org/wiki/The_Jerry_Springer_Show. (Retrieved 2/1/2010).

WHAT YOU SEE IS – WHAT YOU GET!511

NAPHTALI

CHAPTER ELEVEN

---

511 Based on the author's interpretation of Numbers Chapters 13 & 14 of the Bible.

There are some who see the glass as half empty and others who see the glass as half full. Then, there are those who see billions of glasses, overflowing despite the masses that see only one glass, be it half full or half empty. Why is there such a great disparity in perceptions?

It all comes down to what you believe. Do you believe God can or do you believe He can't? That's what it all comes down to. This resolve, combined with the spiritual gift of "faith," will allow you to see and believe in the unseen. You will see great victories, while others proclaim apparent defeat.

What you see is what you get. If you see defeat, negativity, and impossibilities, then you will reap what you sow.

Back in the milk and honey days, the Israelites were in the wilderness, when the Lord spoke to Moses . . . I repeat, the Lord spoke to Moses:

> **Moses, you remember that milk and honey land I've been screaming[512] about. Well congratulations young man, we're here. I want you to send twelve spies to the land known as Canaan. This is the land that I am giving to the children of Israel. Each tribe will elect a leader of their fathers to serve as a spy.**

By the commandment of the Lord, Moses sent:

Spy	Father	Tribe
Shammua	Zaccur	Reuben
Shaphat	Hori	Simeon
Caleb	Jephunneh	Judah
Igal	Joseph	Issachar
Hosea	Nun	Ephraim
Palti	Raphu	Benjamin
Gaddiel	Sodi	Zebulun

---

512   "talking"

Gaddi	Susi	Manassa (A Tribe of Joseph)
Ammiel	Gemalli	Dan
Sethur	Michael	Asher
Nahbi	Vophsi	Naphtali
Geuel	Maki	Gad

The spies became affectionately known as the "Milk and Honey 12" and were proudly displayed before the congregation. Then, an interesting thing happened. God said:

Hey Moses, BTW[513], you know that "Hosea" kid, Nun's boy. I want you to change his name. From hence forward, his name shall be known as "Joshua."

After the name change, Moses gave the spies specific instructions:

We are so proud of you and our prayers are with you. I want you to check[514] the milk and honey land out. Be bold, be strong, and be faithful. If I recall correctly, this is the first season of the ripe grapes. Bring us back a cluster.

Go south into the mountains; see what the land is like; are the people strong or weak; are they few or many; is the land good or bad; are the towns unwalled or fortified; is the land rich or poor; are there lots of trees; in other words, "Get me the 411."[515]

Moses blessed the "Milk and Honey 12;" they said their farewells; and they began their trek into the mountains and wilderness.

The Milk and Honey 12 were seen late into the night marching up the mountains in a single file line. Caleb was leading the line, closely followed by Joshua.

---

513 "By The Way"
514 "inspect"
515 "information; low down; skinny"

In their adventure, the Milk and Honey 12 came upon different, exotic, and treacherous lands. They went up into the hills of Negeb, and down to the valley of Hebron. They searched the lands of Ahiman and Sheshai.

But it was not until they reached Talmai, that they encountered their first real test, the "Anakites." The Anakites were really tall, really strong and really fierce. There was this one guy who struck uncontainable fear in their hearts. He towered among the towers and was the gargantuan among the gargantuans. They called him "Goliath" and, boy did the name fit.

The Milk and Honey 12 observed closely and silently retreated with their report. After spying on the Anakites, they came to the Wadi Eschol (nicknamed the "Wadi Wadi") and they were floored.[516] As far as the eye could see there were clusters and clusters of first season ripe grapes just as Moses had spoken. But these weren't just season grapes. When I say that they were heavy, they were heavy. It took three men to cut a single cluster of Wadi Wadi grapes and two men to carry it on a pole.

They also saw the most righteous pomegranates and figs. *Like they say in real estate, location, location, location.* Wadi Eschcol was put on the map forever.

After forty days and forty nights, Moses, Aaron and the entire Israelite congregation waited with bated breath. Over the mountains, a small figure appeared. As the figure came closer, it was actually the Milk and Honey 12, marching home in a single line.

It's them, it's them. The Milk and Honey 12 have returned. What are those two men carrying? Is it an Ox? What is it? OMG[517], they are grapes. We're gonna[518] party tonight!

The people gathered and Moses and Aaron slowly and methodically moved to the front of the crowd. The Milk and Honey 12 showed the

---

516 "overwhelmed"
517 "Oh My God"
518 "going to"

people the cluster of grapes and everyone marveled, oooed and awed.

Moses, we got the "411." We spied on the land as you asked and, yes, it does indeed flow with milk and honey, and this is its fruit. The two men raised the cluster of grapes and the people shouted almost uncontrollably in anticipation of its sweet nectar. Moses quieted the people, and the spy continued:

But the people who live in the land are strong; the towns are large and fortified; and, that's not the worst of it! Do you remember the Anakites? Well, they live in this milk and honey land, in the land of Negeb.

Immediately, the congregation's hearts were gripped with fear and paralysis. You could literally see the wave of inconsolable panic move across the congregation. The Israelites had only heard about the Anakites, but no one had ever seen them.

By now, the people had forgotten about the "sweet nectar," but the story gets worse. One of the Milk and Honey 12 shouted, *"And don't forget to tell them about the Hittites, the Jebusites, and the Amorites who live in the hill country; and the Canaanites who live by the sea and along the Jordan.*

Somewhere in the back of the congregation, an elderly woman yelled: *"Well, thanks a lot for the favorable report. Is there anyone who doesn't live in this milk and honey land?"*

Moses was astonished and mindlessly pondered in space, repeatedly saying, *"But I know the Lord told me that this was the land of milk and honey. I know it."*

But before Moses could speak, Caleb quieted the people and said, *"Let us go up at once and occupy it, for we are well able to overcome it."*

The other spies looked at Caleb like he had completely taken leave of his senses. *"Caleb, don't you remember? We saw the Anakites, the Hittites, the Amorites and the Canaanites. How many more "ites" do you need to*

understand that we can't do this? They're stronger than we are."

Another spy yelled in a supportive voice: *Don't you remember that giant they called Goliath? He can crush you like a grape.* Caleb was even more inspired and said, "*. . . as a matter of fact, let's go take them now while they're sleeping.*"

So, what we once knew as the Milk and Honey 12, is now the "Milk and Honey 11 formerly known as the 12." After searching the hills and the wilderness, the Milk and Honey 11 brought the Israelites an unfavorable report:

"The land we surveyed is a land that devours its inhabitants and the people were tall, big and wide. Did we mention the Anakites? Well, we think they grew a couple of more feet. They were so big that we seemed like grasshoppers!

Upon hearing this news, the Congregation went mad. Moses, *what the hell are you thinking? You want us to fight the "ites?" Are you crazy?*

After realizing their inevitable end, the people cried all night long. Then, the whole congregation said:

Moses, if we knew this was going to happen, we could have died in Egypt. Hell, we could have died in this wilderness. Why would the Lord bring us this far just to have us fall by the sword? Our wives and our children will become slaves.

All of a sudden, a voice of "reason" emerged from the crowed, "*Hey, wait a minute, I got an idea. We can go back to Egypt, ask Pharaoh for his forgiveness; and work extra hard to build his monuments and pyramids.* The congregation confirmed: *Great idea! Let's choose a captain, and go back to Egypt.*"

Wow! This is amazing. The Israelites wanted to go back to the lash of Pharaoh's whip, instead of following God. Let's not forget. These are the same people who saw Moses transition from the Prince of Egypt; to

a Hebrew Slave; to God's messenger among messengers. These are the same people who saw the ten plagues; the Red Sea depart and collapse to destroy Pharaoh's army; received manna from heaven for food in the wilderness; and followed God by a cloud during the day and a pillar of fire at night!

After all of these miracles, protection and provisions, the Israelites now concluded that God was incapable of conquering Goliath, the Anakites and all of the remaining "ites." The Milk and Honey 11 gave a bad report.

Wait a minute, is this a test? Exactly, it's a test At last, there is a bright star in the class. And the real question is, "What do you believe?" Do you believe God can or do you believe He can't?

Ah, don't be so hard on the Israelites. If you think about it, we're really not so different today. We look at our insignificant problems and act as if God is incapable of providing an answer. We fret and worry when the "right" answer doesn't come immediately.

Yeah, I hear you talking, but at least the Israelites had the advantage of seeing God's miracles. I ain't never seen no Red Sea part; I ain't never seen no Pillar of Fire; and I sure ain't be gotten no manna from heaven.[519]

True, true, I must agree, because, I too, have never seen nor experienced the aforementioned. But, I have seen God hold His hand against a hurricane wind and protect my family from a collapsing building. I have seen family and friends survive medical inevitabilities despite doctors' terminal reports. But most of all, I have personally experienced His goodness, grace and mercy, in spite of all of my filthy ways. God has never stopped being in the miracle business. He's still doing what He always does. He can't help it. He's God, all by himself.

In spite of the Israelites first hand miracle experiences, they still did not believe God could give them the milk and honey land He promised.

---

519   and I definitely did not receive any manna"

Moses and Aaron were astonished at the people and they fell on their faces. Meanwhile, while the people were trippin,[520] Caleb pulled Joshua aside.

Caleb: *"Joshua, you know all that our God has done. You were there from the beginning. You know that we can do this"*

Joshua: *"You're right! I was going to speak up, but I couldn't believe what was coming from our comrades' mouths. I was completely speechless. Dog, I'm wit chu one hundred.*[521]

Then, Joshua and Caleb spoke to the congregation:

Look at the grapes. Do you see how fat[522] they are? We would have brought back more, except we couldn't carry them all and, we were trying to travel light. This is a good land and, more importantly, it is our land.

With God's favor, we can possess and embrace the land that flows with milk and honey. I only ask two things:

    1.   *Do not rebel against the Lord and*
    2.   *Do not fear the people of the land.*

Joshua and Caleb went on to say: *the "ites" are nothing more than bread for us to dip in pure olive oil and consume with the greatest of ease. They have no protection. Our God is with us and for us. We are invincible. The Lord is with us, we promise you. Do not fear them!*

As Joshua and Caleb spoke, some of the congregation looked at them cock eyed. That is, turning your head sideways with body language that says:

---

520   "acting crazy"
521   My good friend, we have an alliance and I support you in full effect.
522   "large"

Are you out of your absolute, 40-day, mountain-climbing, I-don't-care-about-the-grapes-mind? Did you hear what they said? The Anakites live there. Fool, why are you pretending that you didn't hear that?

In spite of their protest, Joshua and Caleb remained steadfast. Then, the whole congregation started looking around for some good throwing stones, because, most of the time, you only get one shot at the apple. They heard enough from these two and a good stoning was the perfect answer to solve this insolence.

In perfect timing, the glory of the Lord appeared to the entire congregation and said:

"How long will you people despise me? How long will you refuse to believe in me, in spite of all the signs that I have done among you? I truly have an idea from God, why don't I strike you down with pestilence and disinherit you. Then, I will make a greater and mightier nation.

What else do you want me to do? I saved you from Pharaoh and you're not happy. I make it so that you roam the wilderness and, for some strange reason, obviously unbeknownst to you, your clothes never tare. I show you all kinds of wonders and sights never seen by man. And you know what, you still don't believe!

You don't deserve My love and protection. I shall strike you down with the mere thought of blinking my eye and I will find another people who are truly worthy of My love. I otta knock you in the head with a case of the bubonic plague right now!

Man, oh Man! God has really had enough. But then again, can you really blame Him? Thank God that He always provides an intercessor. This time the intercessor was Moses. Moses said:

Lord, if you strike them, not me, but them down, then the Egyptians will hear the news and flip[523] the story. They have heard that you are in the midst of your people. You are seen face to face, and Your cloud stands over and leads us. We follow You as a cloud in the day and a pillar of fire by night.

If you destroy your people, then the nations who have heard about You will say: "He ain't be all that bad. He ain't the real God. He probably couldn't give the people the land that He promised, so He killed them as a cover up. He probably was afraid of the legend they called "Goliath."

No, no, no, Lord. Let them remember You as a Lord that is slow to anger and abounding in steadfast love. That You forgive iniquity and transgression, yet, by no means, is this forgiveness interpreted as exoneration.

We know that we have to face the music, but most of all Lord, what about the chillin[524]? Putting the parent's ignant[525] behavior upon the children just ain't right. Even to the third and the fourth generation?

Come on now, Lord you know that ain't right. Don't get me wrong, I know that you're God and everything, but if you can't do it for the parents, can you at least do it for the chillin[526]?

Then, the Lord said:

Moses, that's pretty good. I gotta give it to you. Actually I did because I knew you were going to say it before the earth was created.

I will forgive, just as you have asked. But don't think that

---

523 "change"
524 "children"
525 "ignorant"
526 "children"

it's going to be that easy. **As I live, and as all the earth is filled with My glory, and it is, not one single knucklehead has obeyed my voice. The most amazing thing is they chose to dis[527] me, even after they have seen all of my glory and signs.**

Do I get any respect? Nahhhh, instead, they dis[528] me over and over and over again. All that I have heard is:

- *I ordered my manna well done and it was medium rare. What kind of joint are you running here!*
- *My manna was cooked with ham hocks and I don't eat pork flavored manna!*
- *I've been tracking all over the wilderness in these same ugly brown leather sandals and everybody knows that the new Gucci sandals are the latest.*

Then, God said:

Ten times these people have disrespected me and not obeyed my voice. Not one of you bone heads shall see the milk and honey land I promised. Remember the land I swore to your ancestors. Yeah, those same fat clusters of grapes that you oooed and awed about . . . GONE, FINITE, CAPUTE, SIANARA, NADA, NATHAN[529].

While all you were crying about your doom and gloom, my servant Caleb was creating a military strategy to overcome. Why, because he believes. He is of a different spirit.

When he saw the Anakites, he followed me wholeheartedly and knew, with God, all things and people are conquerable. Because Caleb believed, I will

---

527 "Disrespect"
528 *Id.*
529 "Gone beyond gone"

bring him and his descendants shall possess the milk and honey land. Well, since you fear the Anakites so much, tomorrow, we'll start our wilderness adventure by way of the Red Sea.

Then the Lord, Moses and Aaron truly, in every sense of the word, had a "come to Jesus meeting."[530]

I mean business this time. This ill-mannered bunch shall fall dead in this very wilderness. Remember that census, I had you take? Yeah the one you guys thought was of no value . . . well it has value now. Every person, except Caleb, son of Jephunneh; Joshua, son of Nun; and their descendents shall fall dead in this wilderness.

Tell the Israelite congregation that today is reverse day. Their children will not become slaves. Oh nooo! Their children shall enslave many people and inherit the milk and honey land I promised.

But, as for the parents, their bodies shall fall dead in this wilderness and their children shall bear the spiritual, emotional and physical burden of their parents' death. The children will bury their parents' bodies knowing that they cannot cross the Jordan river into the land of milk and honey until after the last body falls dead.

Before you get all riled up, it's not going to be that bad. It's not forever. Since I sent the spies to explore the land for forty days; forty shall be the magic number that my people shall roam the wilderness.

---

530 "Come to Jesus meeting" means to have the most serious of discussions about the most serious subjects. To bring resolve and finality.

Moses and Aaron were relieved. *"Forty days, that's not so bad. We can deal with that."* But then the Lord said:

Forty days? Wrong Answer! Forty years! One year for each day the land was spied. For forty years, you shall bear your iniquity and know my displeasure.

I am the Lord all by myself. I have spoken and surely I will fulfill my word with this wicked congregation. The wilderness shall truly separate the wheat from the chaff. Peace out! [531]

Moses was grateful for God sparing the congregation, but his heart was heavy. So many people would never see the milk and honey land, because they didn't believe.

Moses was walking endlessly in circles, trying to find the words to tell the people about the forty year trek when he caught a glimpse of the ten spies that brought the unfavorable report. Immediately, his heart fell further into the abyss, because the Lord had stricken them with a plague.

After the congregation heard the news, they wailed bitterly in the streets, constantly trying to console each other, while simultaneously pondering their own fate. Occasionally, they would look at their children and begin to weep uncontrollably.

After the bitterness and sorrow, came the hateration. [532] *"Yeah, I know that we made a mistake, but we're only human. So what, that Caleb and Joshua spoke up this time? What about all of the other times? I don't remember hearing their voices when we had the golden calf incident."*

Just then, Caleb and Joshua overheard the hater's conversation and responded:

---

531 "Good bye" "So it is said, so it is written"
532 "jealousy"

"Why is there so much hateration[533] in the hizouse[534]? You're so busy hating on us that you completely forgot about your own fate. We all climbed the same mountains; we all searched the same valleys; and we all helped to cut down and carry the Wadi Wadi grapes

You saw unconquerable lands and formidable foes; whereas, we saw ourselves possessing and taking the land. You saw giants; whereas, we saw ants. You saw Goliath and compared him to man. We saw Goliath and compared him to God. **What you see is what you get!"**

Wow! Kinda of makes you want to speak up next time and see life through a different lens. What made Caleb and Joshua so different? What made them so special? The answer is apparent. *They passed the test.*

Caleb and Joshua chose not to focus on the Anakites, but to see what God had promised. Caleb and Joshua held God to his word and believed. They believed if God sent them to survey the land, then He must have wanted them to possess it. Instead of seeing the challenges, they saw His wonders; His goodness; and His favor.

Every day is a test and again, the most important questions are: "What do you see" and "What do you believe?"

If you see:

- I can't do it
- It's impossible
- No one in my family has ever tried

then you will receive:

- Failure
- Lack of Vision
- Generational Curses

---

533 "jealousy and envy"
534 'house"

- Lack of Identity
- Insecurity
- Lack of Self-Esteem

But if you see:

- I can do all things through Christ who strengthens me[535]
- I am God's Special Child and God cannot fail
- God grants me favor because I believe

Then, "all things" includes "taxes" also and you will receive:

- God's abundant tax blessings
- God's tax protection and
- God's tax favor.

What you see is what you get? I beseeched you to see faithfully; believe God can; and know that God will. Amen.

---

535   Philippians 4:13 KJV

REVELATION

GAD

CHAPTER TWELVE

Several years ago, I adopted my current mantra . . . "If I wake up in the morning, then it's a **_good_** day. If God chooses to wake my family up, then it's a **_great_** day. If what I encounter during the day doesn't kill me, it must have made me stronger."

Entrepreneurs are nothing more than legitimate hustlers. Every day we must "fish or cut bait" and "cutting bait" don't sound like too much fun to me. Every entrepreneur has the same fundamental rule: *"You eat what you kill!"*

As an entrepreneur, there is no sick leave and there is no sleeping late. You must get your hustle on every day and night for your clients and your family.

One morning, I was scheduled to speak to an event sponsored by a local County's Chamber of Commerce. After showering and praying, I went to the closet to get suited up. Damn! I've been burning the candle on both ends and in the middle and I neglected to drop off my clothes at the cleaners.

My only options were a black suit and a black pinstriped shirt. Beggars can't be choosey, so I pulled down a gray silk tie and got dressed.

After taking a look at the man in the mirror and insuring that all was in place, I began to look at the forest and the trees, I immediately thought, *"You can't speak looking like this . . . You look like some kind of Gangsta!"* Then it hit me – "Revelation" – *I am a Gangsta and "it is, what it is."*

That's right, *"it is, what it is."* If the IRS is the Original Gangsta, then there are rules that govern its syndicate. The Mafia is a lifetime membership. The Mafia has Godfathers, families, hit men and hit women, accountants, and its own security force. Truly till death do you part!

As a former Consigliore for the Original Gangsta, I have come to realize, I too, am a Gangsta. I remember going on a golfing trip one year and the fellas were discussing guerilla warfare. The question was poised, "How do you defeat a guerilla?" And the answer was simple, "Become a guerilla." Hence, it is impossible to fight a Gangsta and not be a Gangsta!

Being trained in their ways, I served as a valve in the malignant heart of the collection chamber we know as the IRS a.k.a[536] "The Original Gangsta." Its ways are my ways. Its thoughts are my thoughts. The Original Gangsta is undeniably apart of me and I apart of it.

And in all honesty, my heart is probably still tainted with the smudges of the Original Gangsta's black, crusty, ashy heart. How else could I possibly stand up to them everyday? *That's a good question; does the IRS even have a heart?*

The only difference between me and "The Original Gangsta" is I've been given permission to serve as Consigliore for the people. I am a brain for the people, not the syndicate. My sole purpose is to set God's people free from the mental and emotional bondage of tax slavery.

As Minister of Tax, I feel like a man on a secluded island. I don't truly fit with most attorneys and I definitely don't fit with the accountants. I continue to follow this calling with the sole purpose of helping God's people through this maniacal tax maze.

Who are God's people, you ask? Like they say at the Hard Rock Café . . . "Love all, Serve all."[537] I'm a nomad roaming the country in a camel hair blazer with a leather belt. Much like, yes, I would say, very much like, John the Baptist.

---

536 "also known as"

537 Hard Rock Cafe is a chain of <u>restaurants</u> founded in London (1971) by two Americans: <u>Peter Morton</u> & <u>Isaac Tigrett</u>. In 1979, the Hard Rock Cafe began covering its walls with <u>rock and roll memorabilia</u>, a tradition which expanded to other chains. In 2007, Hard Rock was sold to the <u>Seminole Tribe of Florida</u>, and is headquartered in <u>Orlando, Florida</u>. Currently, there are one hundred and fifty (150) Hard Rock locations in 53 countries with the largest in Orlando. *See* Hard Rock Cafe - Wikipedia, the free encyclopedia. (<u>http://en.wikipedia.org/wiki/Hard_Rock_Cafe</u>)(Retrieved May 1, 2012)

As the Minister of Tax, my calling is to spread the good word and not only proclaim, "Repent, Repent For the Savior is Nigh." But also, encouraging you to "Tithe;" "Get Your Mind Right;" "Pay Attention To The Man Behind the Curtain;" and "Render Unto Caesar That Which Is Caesar's; But Nothing More."

Trust me! The only way to beat the system is to work from within armed with faith and knowledge. The longer I practice, the greater I am exposed to unbelievable atrocities. Yet, in spite of the challenges, I am bound to answer my calling until God is finished.

As I was writing this book, I asked God, *"What do you want me to tell Your people?"* "He said, **"Tell them that I love them, and if they turn away from their wicked ways, then I will bless them, their land, and their seed."**

I submit that turning away from our wicked ways includes: returning prayer to school; standing up for right; and knowing that we are His children so we can not fail. Don't trip![538] Being and believing takes courage, stamina, and conjones. What happens when you're faced with the decision to trust God and release the reins? Do you have the umph and faith to say "okay" and know that it's gonna be alright. It ain't easy. But, boy is it rewarding! *True dat!*[539]

Because taxes are so complicated and stressing, my office is designed to make our clients feel comfortable. After consultations, our clients feel as though a burden has been lifted and they sigh with relief. Well, that burden is shifted from the clients' shoulders to our laps.

Sometimes, there are small fires and, many times, the fires are conflagrations. Nonetheless, there are fires everyday and we put on our fire hats, amp up the analytical professional skills, and pray.

Many times the conflagrations have been so huge that we can't do anything, except call upon the Mighty Name of Jesus. I recall one

---

538 "Please don't misunderstand me"
539 "Most definitely"

day in particular. I entered the familiar lobby of the Original Gangsta and requested to see Revenue Officer Taylor. She briskly opened the electronically locked door and asked me to follow her.

As I walk pass the cubicles, I politely spoke:

- *Good Morning Mr. Rogers, we'll have that information for you by Friday.*
- *Good Morning Ms. Lebowitz, did you receive our fax?*
- *Good Morning Mr. Dale, we'll make sure and respond within the allotted time. Thank you.*

One after another, I greeted each agent, knowing that the day may come when I am escorted to their cubicle. So far, so good!

After becoming situated, I politely ask:

Ms. Taylor, may I plug my telephone into an outlet for charging?

No, you can't! You are here to provide me with information regarding this tax situation and I will decide whether it's persuasive and compliant.

Ooooh Wee! I can see that we're going to have fun tonight. *Ms. Taylor, u be de juge, jurie and cherif.*[540] Remember, audits are sky rocketing like nobody's business and word has gotten out that we "handle my business."[541]

We proceed with the audit. I am sitting on the edge of the seat listening and analyzing Ms. Taylor's questions, responses, and body language. They say that body language is seventy percent (70%) of communication and so far, it ain't[542] looking too good.

Oh, by the way, Ms. Taylor, we would like to employ the forty

---

540 Mrs. Taylor, you are the judge, jury and sheriff.
541 Fight the Internal Revenue Service tooth and nail.
542 "isn't"

(40) year depreciation, instead of the 27.5.

You can't do that and I won't allow it.

Why?

I'm not too sure, I must consult legal counsel.

At this point, I am confused. You're definitively denying the request, even though you've admitted your ignorance of the law. I'm doing my best to keep my cool because don't forget, Ms. Taylor *"b de juge, jurie and cherif."*[543]

Maintaining a polite tone, and controlling my body language, I ask:

> *Ms. Taylor, may I use your Internal Revenue Code and Regulations?*

No, you may not!

Oh my God, I can't even use "The Original Gangsta's" books issued to Ms. Taylor free of cost. During Al Capone's time, the Tommy Gun[544] was standard issue. Well, for "The Original Gangsta's" employees, the Internal Revenue Code and Regulations are standard issue. The only difference is these resources are public information and everybody has access to them. Ms. Taylor ain't be[545] playing fair.

In spite of the fact that Ms. Taylor has probably never read the Internal Revenue Code . . . *I can't use it!* I was absolutely floored.

The audit continued and I was fairly certain that Ms. Taylor was wasting our time, because this case is going to appeals. As we conclude, she remarked:

---

543 *Supra.*
544 *See* American Submarine Gun, *Supra* cited at Footnote 136.
545 "isn't"

I'm glad this is coming to an end, so I don't have to see you anymore. Here's your information.

As I looked at her in amazement, I just couldn't control myself. As unprofessional as it sounds, I told Ms. Taylor, "*I feel exactly the same way!*" Wow, you really told her.

As I was driving back to the office marinating over the entire audit, I realized that Ms. Taylor wasn't interested in analysis, evidence, or truth. Her sole objective was to subjectively find any flaw, legal or imagined, to deny our clients' rightful tax claim.

Could Ms. Taylor really be that mean? Why? Couldn't she see that the taxpayers were victims of the real estate debacle? When I got back to the office, I was hot, angry, perplexed, and ready to "*chrome and metal it.*"[546]

In my anger, I stated, "***Jesus, I can't believe these freaking people. They are gangsta taxing not only without representation, but without any regard, respect or remorse. More so, they've got attitude to boot. Jesus is definitely not up in the camp***[547]." Just then, my office manager Mrs. Tillman knew that I was writing a book and she leaped out of her seat and said, that's it "*Jesus Don't*[548] *Work For The IRS.*"

The End

---

546   "Pull out the guns and start blazing (shooting)."
547   "is not recognized in this abode or office"
548   "Doesn't"

Upcoming Chapters

- "The Fair Tax" – Is It Really Fair"

- You Say "Potato;" I Say "Potatoe",[549] You say "Employee," I say "Independent Contractor."

- The Original Gangsta – Alternative Ending

- Hater's Never Prosper and Prospers Never Hate

- Limited Liability Company vs. S-Corporation vs. C-Corporation vs. Partnership. Who the hell knows, who the hell cares?

- The "N" Word

- And He woke up the next morning.

- Running for Jesus!

---

549   Lyrics paraphrased from "Let's Call the Whole Thing Off." Written by George Gershwin and Ira Gershwin for the 1937 film "Shall We Dance." (http://en.wikipedia.org/wiki/Let%27s_Call_The_Whole_Thing_Off) (Retrieved 3/20/2012).